THE OX TEAM
or
THE OLD OREGON TRAIL

An Account of the Author's Trip Across The Plains, from the Missouri River to Puget Sound, at the Age of Twenty-two, With an Ox and Cow Team in 1852, And Of His Return with an Ox Team in the Year 1906, at the Age of Seventy-six, with Copious Excerpts From His Journal and Other Reliable Sources of Information; A Narrative of Events and Descriptive of Present and Past Conditions

by
Ezra Meeker

The Ox Team or The Old Oregon Trail was originally published by the author in 1906.

Book design and layout (c) 2025 by Firebird Creative.
This edition was produced by Firebird Creative, LLC (Clackamas, OR).

THE OX TEAM
or
THE OLD OREGON TRAIL

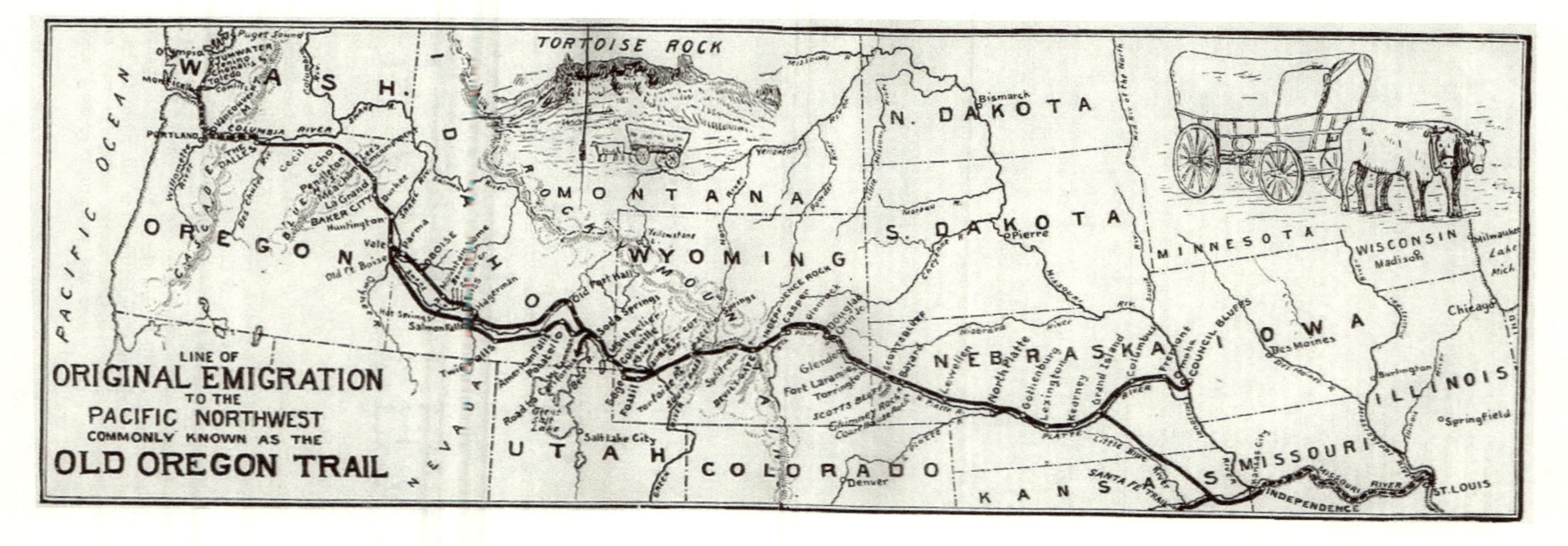
LINE OF
ORIGINAL EMIGRATION
TO THE
PACIFIC NORTHWEST
COMMONLY KNOWN AS THE
OLD OREGON TRAIL
PACIFIC OCEAN
TORTOISE ROCK
WASH.
OREGON
IDAHO
MONTANA
WYOMING
N. DAKOTA
S. DAKOTA
NEBRASKA
MINNESOTA
IOWA
WISCONSIN
ILLINOIS
MISSOURI
KANSAS
COLORADO
UTAH
NEVADA
Portland
Columbia River
The Dalles
Echo
Pendleton
La Grande
Baker City
Huntington
Vale
Boise
Parma
Hagerman
Old Fort Hall
Soda Springs
Pocatello
Salt Lake City
Independence Rock
Casper
Douglas
Fort Laramie
Torrington
Scotts Bluff
Bayard
Lewellen
North Platte
Gothenburg
Lexington
Kearney
Grand Island
Columbus
Fremont
Omaha
Council Bluffs
Des Moines
Bismarck
Pierre
Madison
Chicago
Springfield
Denver
Kansas City
Independence
St. Louis
Santa Fe Trail
Missouri River

THE OLD OREGON TRAIL

THIS FAMOUS TRAIL, the natural gateway to the Pacific, may be said to date back to the discovery of the South Pass of the Rocky Mountains in 1822 by Etienne Provost, although sections of it had been traversed by hardy adventurers in the early part of the seventeenth century.

After the buffaloes came the Indians, followed in turn by trappers and traders, and these by the intrepid missionaries who pointed the way for that mightiest migration of the world's history, the home builders, of the Pacific Northwest, to the Oregon country. History does not record so great a movement for so great a distance as this, over a 2,000 miles stretch of an unknown country from the Missouri River to the Pacific coast. The Mormons in 1846 and the gold seekers of California in '49 followed the Oregon Trail for more than a thousand miles to the big bend of the Bear River and contended for possession of the single trail then existing, with the still passing throng to Oregon, until in later years parallel tracks were worn deep for long distances as the multitudes jostled each other on their weary westward journey.

The Oregon Trail is without its parallel of picturesque sceneries, its tragedies and legends of heroism, that some day will lend a theme for an imperishable epic to go down into history for all ages, as has already been the physical marks along the way to point the spots where the multitudes passed and suffered and died.

The Dream of the Star

*[A Song of the Oregon Trail.
Dedicated to Ezra Meeker, pioneer.]*

I

*A song for the men who blazed the way!
With hearts that would not quail
They made brave quest of the wild Northwest.
They cut the Oregon trail.*

*Back of them beckoned their kith and kin
And all that they held their own;
Front of them spread the wilderness dread.
And ever the vast unknown.*

*But ever they kept their forward course.
And never they thought to lag.
For over them flew the Red, White and Blue
And the dream of a star for the flag!*

II

*A cheer for the men who cut the trail!
With souls as firm as steel
And fiery as wrath they hewed the path
For the coming Commonweal.*

*And close on the heels of the pioneers
The eager throng closed in
And followed the road to a far abode.
An Empire new to win.*

*And so they wrought at the end of the trail,
As ever must brave men do.
Till out of the dark there gleamed a spark.
And the dream of the star came true!*

III

A toast to the men who made the road!
And a health to the men who dwell
In the great new land by the heroes planned,
Who have builded it wide and well!

The temple stands where the pine tree stood.
And dim is the ancient trail.
But many and wide are the roads that guide
And stanch are the ships that sail!

For the land is a grand and goodly land.
And its fruitful fields are tilled
By the sons who see on the flag of the free
The dream of the star fulfilled!

—ROBERTUS LOVE

DEDICATION

To the Pioneers who fought the battle of peace, and wrested Oregon from British rule, this book is reverently dedicated.

INTRODUCTION TO AN INTRODUCTION

I had not, until the last moment, intended to write an introduction, unless my readers accepted the writing of early Indiana life as such. Introductions so often take the form of an apology that the dear public properly omits to read them, and so I will content myself with the remark that this reference to my first chapter shall answer for the Introduction, for which I offer no apology.

CHAPTER I

FROM INDIANA TO IOWA
EARLY DAYS IN INDIANA

IN THE EARLY '50s, out four and a half and seven miles respectively from Indianapolis, Indiana, there lived two young people with their parents, who were old-time farmers of the old style, keeping no "hired man" nor buying many "store goods." The girl could spin and weave, make delicious butter, knit soft, good shapen socks, and cook as good a meal as any other country girl around about, and withal as buxom a lass as had ever been "born and raised there (Indiana) all her life."

These were times when sugar sold for eighteen cents per pound, calico fifteen cents per yard, salt three dollars a barrel, and all other goods at these comparatively high prices, while butter would bring but ten cents a pound, eggs five cents a dozen, and wheat but two bits (twenty-five cents) a bushel. And so, when these farmers went to the market town (Indianapolis) care was taken to carry along something to sell, either some eggs or butter or perhaps a half dozen pairs of socks, or maybe a few yards of cloth, as well as some grain, or hay or a bit of pork, or possibly a load of wood, to make ends meet at the store.

The young man was a little uncouth in appearance, round-faced, rather stout in build—almost fat—a little boisterous, always restless, and without a very good address, yet with at least one redeeming trait of character: he loved his work and was known as industrious a lad as any in the neighborhood.

THE BRIMSTONE MEETING-HOUSE

These young people would sometimes meet at the "Brimstone meeting-house," a Methodist church known by that name far and wide; so named by the unregenerate because of the open preaching of endless torment to follow nonchurch members and sinners to the grave—a literal lake of fire, taught with vehemence and accompanied with boisterous scenes of shouting of those who were "saved." Amid these scenes and these surroundings these two young people grew up to the age of manhood and womanhood, knowing but little of the world outside of their home sphere—and who knows but as happy as if they had seen the whole world? Had they not experienced the joys of the sugar camp while "stirring off" the lively creeping maple sugar? Both had been thumped upon the bare head by the falling hickory nuts in windy weather; had hunted the black walnuts half hidden in the leaves; had scraped the ground for the elusive beach nuts, had even ventured to apple parings together, though not yet out of their "teens." The lad hunted the 'possum and the coon in the White River bottom, now the suburb of the city of Indianapolis, and had cut even the stately walnut trees, now so valuable (extinct in fact) that the cunning coon might be driven from his hiding place.

I'M GOING TO BE A FARMER

"I'm going to be a farmer when I get married," the young man quite abruptly said one day to the lass, without any previous conversation to lead up to such an assertion, to the confusion of his companion, who could not mistake the thoughts that prompted the words. A few months later the lass said, "Yes, I want to be a farmer, too, but I want to be a farmer on our own land," and two bargains were confirmed then and there when the lad said, "We will go west and not live on pap's farm." "Nor in the old cabin, nor any cabin unless it's our own," came the response, and so the resolution was made that they would go to Iowa, get some land, and grow up with the country.

OFF FOR IOWA

About the first week of October, 1851, a covered wagon drew up in front of Thomas Sumner's habitation, then but four miles out from Indianapolis on the National road, ready to be loaded for the start. Eliza Jane, the second daughter of that noble man, the "lass" described, then the wife of the young man mentioned, the author, was ready, with cake and apple butter and pumpkin pies, jellies and the like, enough to last the whole trip and plenty besides. Not much of a load, to be sure, but it was all we had: plenty of blankets, a good old-fashioned feather bed, a good sized Dutch oven, and each an extra pair of shoes and cloth for two new dresses for the wife, and for an extra pair of pants for the husband.

Tears could be restrained no longer as the loading progressed and the stem realization faced the parents of both that the young couple were about to leave them.

"Why, mother, we are only going out to Iowa, you know, where we can get a home that shall be our own; it's not so very far—only about 500 miles."

"Yes, I know, but suppose you get sick in that uninhabited country—who will care for you?"

Notwithstanding this motherly solicitude, the young people could not fail to know there was a secret feeling of approval in the good woman's breast, and when, after a few miles' travel, the reluctant final parting came, could not then know that this loved parent would lay down her life a few years later in an heroic attempt to follow the wanderers to Oregon, and that her bones would rest in an unknown and unmarked grave of the Platte valley.

Of that October drive from the home near Indianapolis to Eddyville, Iowa, in the delicious (shall I say delicious, for what other word expresses it?) atmosphere of an Indian summer, and in the atmosphere of hope and content; hope born of aspirations—content with our lot, born of a confidence for the future, what shall I say? What matter if we had but a few dollars in money and but few belongings; we had the wide world before us; we had good health; and before and above all we had each other and were supremely happy, and rich in our anticipations.

At that time but one railroad entered Indianapolis—it would be called a tramway now— from Madison on the Ohio river, and when we cut loose from that embryo city we left railroads behind us, except such as were found in the wagon track where the rails were laid crossways to keep the wagon out of the mud. What matter if the road was rough, we could go a little slower, and then would not we have a better appetite for our supper because of the jolting, and wouldn't we sleep a little sounder for it? And so everything in all the world looked bright, and what little mishaps did befall us were looked upon with light hearts, that they might have been worse.

The great Mississippi river was crossed at Burlington, or, rather, we embarked several miles down the river and were carried up to the landing at Burlington, and after a few days' further driving landed in Eddyville, Iowa, destined to be only a place to winter, and a way station on our route to Oregon.

AN IOWA WINTER

My first introduction to an Iowa winter was in a surveyor's camp on the western borders of the state, a little way north of Kanesville (now Council Bluffs), as cook of the party, which position was speedily changed and that of flagman assigned me.

If there are any settlers now left of the Iowa of that day (fifty-five years ago) they will remember the winter was bitter cold—the coldest within the memory of the oldest inhabitant. On my trip back from the surveying party just mentioned to Eddyville, just before Christmas, I encountered one of those cold days long to be remembered. A companion named Vance rested with me over night in a cabin, with scant food for ourselves or the mare we led. It was thirtyfive miles to the next cabin; we must reach that place or lay out on the snow. So a very early start was made, before daybreak while the wind lay. The good lady of the cabin baked some biscuits for a noon lunch, but they were frozen solid in our pockets before we had been out two hours. The wind rose with the sun, and with the sun two bright sun-dogs, one on each side, and alongside of each, but slightly less bright, another—a beautiful sight to behold, but arising from conditions intolerable to bear. Vance came near freezing to death, and would had I not succeeded in arousing him to anger and gotten him off the mare.

I vowed then and there I did not like the Iowa climate, and the Oregon fever was visibly quickened. Besides, if I went to Oregon the government gave us 320 acres of land, while in Iowa we would have to purchase it—at a low price, to be sure, but it must be bought and paid for on the spot. There were no preemption or beneficent homestead laws in force then, and not until many years later. The country was a wide open, rolling prairie, a beautiful country indeed—but what about a market? No railroads, no wagon roads, no cities, no meeting-houses, no schools; the prospect looked drear. How easy it is for one when his mind is once bent against a country to conjure up all sorts of reasons to bolster his, perhaps, hasty conclusions; and so Iowa was condemned as unsuited to our life abiding place.

But what about going to Oregon when springtime came? An interesting event was pending that rendered a positive decision impossible for the moment, and not until the first week of April, 1852, when our first-born baby boy was a month old, could we say that we were going to Oregon in 1852.

CHAPTER II

OFF FOR OREGON

I HAVE BEEN asked hundreds of times how many wagons were in the train I traveled with, and what train it was, and who was the captain, assuming that of course we must be with some train.

THE START

When we drove out of Eddyville there was but one wagon in our train, two yoke of four-year-old steers, one yoke of cows, and one extra cow. This cow was the only animal we lost on the whole trip: strayed in the Missouri river bottom before crossing.

And now as to the personnel of our little party. William Buck, who became my partner for the trip, was a man six years my senior, had had some experience on the Plains, and knew well as to an outfit needed, but had no knowledge as to a team of cattle. He was an impulsive man and to some extent excitable, yet withal a man of excellent judgment and as honest as God Almighty makes men. No lazy bone occupied a place in Buck's body. He was so scrupulously neat and cleanly that some might say he was fastidious, but such was not the case. His aptitude for the camp work and unfitness for handling the team, at once, as we might say by natural selection, divided the cares of the household, sending the married man to the range with the team and the bachelor to the camp. The little wife was in ideal health, and almost as "particular" as Buck (not quite though), while the young husband would be a little more on the slouchy order, if the reader will pardon the use of that word, though more expressive than elegant.

Buck selected the outfit to go into the wagon, while I fitted up the wagon and bought the team.

We had butter, packed in the center of the flour in double sacks; eggs packed in corn meal or flour, to last us nearly five hundred miles; fruit in abundance, and dried pumpkins; a little jerked beef, not too salt, and last, a demijohn of brandy for "medicinal purposes only," as he said, with a merry twinkle of the eye that exposed the subterfuge which he knew I knew without any sign. The little wife had prepared the homemade yeast cake which she knew so well how to make and dry, and we had light bread all the way, baked in a tin reflector instead of the heavy Dutch ovens so much in use on the Plains.

Albeit the butter to a considerable extent melted and mingled with the flour, yet we were not much disconcerted as the short-cake that followed made us almost glad the mishap had occurred. Besides, did we not have plenty of fresh butter churned every day in the can, by the jostle of the wagon, from our own cows? Then the buttermilk. What a luxury, yes, that's the word, a real luxury. I will never, so long as I live, forget that short-cake and corn bread, the puddings and pumpkin pies, and above all the buttermilk. The reader who may smile at this may well recall the fact that it is the small things that make up the happiness of life.

But it was more than that. As we gradually crept out on the Plains and saw the sickness and suffering caused by improper food and in some cases from improper preparation, it gradually dawned on me how blessed I was, with such a partner as Buck and such a life partner as the little wife. Some trains, it soon transpired, were without fruit, and most of them depended upon saleratus for raising their bread. Many had only fat bacon for meat till the buffalo supplied a change, and no doubt but much of the sickness attributed to the cholera was caused by an illsuited diet.

I am willing to claim credit for the team, every hoof of which reached the Coast in safety. Four four-year-old steers and two cows were sufficient for our light wagon and light outfit, not a pound of which but was useful (except the brandy, of which more anon) and necessary for our comfort. Not one of these had ever been under the yoke, though plenty of "broke" oxen could be had, but generally of that class that had been broken in spirit as Avell as in training, so, when we got across the river with the cattle strung out to the wagon with Buck on the off side to watch, while I, figuratively speaking, took the reins in hand, we may have presented a ludicrous sight, but did not have time to think whether we did or not, and cared but little so the team would go.

FIRST DAY OUT

The first day's drive out from Eddyville was a short one, and so far as I now remember the only one on the whole trip where the cattle were allowed to stand in the yoke while the owners lunched and rested. I made it a rule, no matter how short the noon time, to unyoke and let the cattle rest or eat while we rested and ate, and on the present 1906 trip have rigidly adhered to that rule.

An amusing scene was enacted when, at near nightfall, the first camp was made. Buck excitedly insisted we must not unyoke the cattle. "Well, what shall we do?" I said; "they can't live in the yoke always; we will have to unyoke them sometimes."

"Yes, but if you unyoke here you will never catch them again." One word brought on another, till the war of words had almost reached the stage of a dispute, when a stranger, Thomas McAuley, who was camped near by, with a twinkle in his eye I often afterwards saw and will always remember, interfered and said his cattle were gentle and there were three men of his party and that they would help us yoke up in the morning. I gratefully accepted his proffered help, speedily unyoked, and ever after that never a word with the merest semblance of contention passed between Buck and myself.

Scanning McAuley's outfit the next morning I was quite troubled to start out with him, his teams being light, principally cows, and thin in flesh, with wagons apparently light and as frail as the teams. But I soon found that his outfit, like ours, contained no extra weight; that he knew how to care for a team; and was withal an obliging neighbor, as was fully demonstrated on many trying occasions, after having traveled in company for more than a thousand miles, and until his road to California parted from ours, at the big bend of Bear river.

Of the trip through Iowa little remains to be said further than that the grass was thin and washy, the roads muddy and slippery, and weather execrable, although May had been ushered in long before we reached the Missouri river.

CHAPTER III

CROSSING THE MISSOURI

WHAT ON EARTH IS THAT?" exclaimed Margaret McAuley as we approached the ferry landing a few miles below where Omaha now stands.

"It looks for all the world like a great big white flatiron," answered Eliza, the sister, "doesn't it, Mrs. Meeker?" But, leaving the women folks to their similes, we drivers turned our attention more to the teams as we encountered the roads "cut all to pieces" on account of the concentrated travel as we neared the landing and the solid phalanx of wagons that formed the flatiron of white ground.

We here encountered a sight indeed long to be remembered. The "flatiron of white" that Eliza had seen proved to be wagons with their tongues pointing to the landing—a center train with other parallel trains extending back in the rear and gradually covering a wider space the farther back from the river one would go. Several hundred wagons were thus closely interlocked, completely blocking the approach to the landing by new arrivals, whether in companies or single. All round about were camps of all kinds, from those without covering of any kind to others with comfortable tents, nearly all seemingly intent on merry-making, while here and there were small groups engaged in devotional services. We soon ascertained these camps contained the outfits in great part of the wagons in line in the great white flatiron, some of whom had been there for two weeks with no apparent probability of securing an early crossing. At the turbulent river front the turbid waters had already swallowed up three victims, one of whom I saw go under the drift of a small island as I stood near his shrieking wife the first day we were there. Two scows were engaged in crossing the wagons and teams. In this case the stock had rushed to one side of the boat, submerged the gunwale, and precipitated the whole contents into the dangerous river. One yoke of oxen, having reached the farther shore, deliberately entered the river with a heavy yoke on and swam to the Iowa side, and were finally saved by the helping hands of the assembled emigrants.

"What should we do?" was passed around, without answer. Tom McAuley was not yet looked upon as a leader, as was the case later. The sister Margaret, a most determined maiden lady, the oldest of the party and as resolute and brave as the bravest, said to build a boat. But of what should we build it? While this question was under consideration and a search for material made, one of our party, who had gotten across the river in search of timber for oars, discovered a scow almost completely buried, on the sand spit opposite the landing, "only just a small bit of the railing and a corner of the boat visible." The report seemed to be too good to be true. The next thing to do was to find the owner, which in a search of a day we did, eleven miles down the river. "Yes, if you will stipulate to deliver the boat safely to me after crossing your five wagons and teams, you can have it," said the owner, and a bargain was closed right then and there. My! but didn't we make the sand fly that night from that boat? By morning we could begin to see the end. Then busy hands began to cut a landing on the perpendicular sandy bank on the Iowa side; others were preparing sweeps, and all was bustle and stir and I might say excitement.

By this time it had become noised around that another boat would be put on to ferry people over, and we were besieged with applications from detained emigrants. Finally, the word coming to the ears of the ferrymen, they were foolish enough to undertake to prevent us from crossing ourselves. A writ of replevin or some other process was issued, I never knew exactly what, directing the sheriff to take possession of the boat when landed and which he attempted to do. I never before nor since attempted to resist an officer of the law, nor joined to accomplish anything by force outside the pale of the law, but when that sheriff put in an appearance and we realized what it meant, there wasn't a man in our party that did not run for his gun to the nearby camp, and it would seem needless to add we did not need to use them. As if by magic a hundred guns were in sight. The sheriff withdrew, and the crossing went peaceably on till all our wagons were safely landed. But we had another danger to face: we came to know there would be an attempt to take the boat from us, not as against us, but against the owner, and but for the adroit management of McAuley and my brother Oliver, who had joined us, we would have been unable to fulfil our engagements with the owner.

CHAPTER IV

OUT ON THE PLAINS
THE INDIANS

AS SOON AS A PART OF OUR OUTFITS were landed on the right bank of the river our trouble with the Indians began, not as in open hostilities, but in robbery under the guise of beggary. The word had been passed around in our little party that not one cent's worth of provisions would we give up to the Indians, believing this policy was our only safeguard from spoliation, and in that we were right. The women folks had been sent over the river with the first wagon, and sent off a little way to a convenient camp, so that the first show of arms came from that side of our little community, when some of the bolder Pawnees attempted to pilfer around the wagons. But no blood was shed, and I may say in passing there was none shed by any of our party during the whole trip, though there did come a show of arms in several instances.

One case in particular I remember. Soon after we hiad left the Missouri river we came to a small bridge over a washout across the road, evidently constructed but very recently by some train just ahead of us. The Indians had taken possession and demanded pay for crossing. Some ahead of us had paid, while others were hesitating, but with a few there was a determined resolution not to pay. When our party came up it remained for that fearless man, McAuley, in quite short order to clear the way though the Indians were there in considerable numbers. McAuley said, "You fellers come right on, for I'm going across that bridge if I have to run right over that Ingen settin' there." And he did almost run over the Indian, who at the last moment got out of the way of his team, which was followed in such quick succession and with such show of arms the Indians withdrew and left the road unobstructed. We did not, however, have much trouble with the Indians in 1852. The facts are the great numbers of the emigrants, coupled with the superiority of their arms, placed them on comparatively safe grounds. And it must be remembered, also, that this was before the treaty-making period, which has so often been followed by bloodshed and war.

But to return to the river bank. We crossed on the 17th and 18th of May and drove out a short way on the 19th, but not far enough to be out of hearing of a shrill steamboat whistle that resounded over the prairie, announcing the arrival of a steamer. I never knew the size of that steamer, or the name, but only know that a dozen wagons or more could be crossed at one time, and that a dozen or more trips could be made during the day, and as many at night, and that we were overtaken by this throng of a thousand wagons thrown upon the road, that gave us some trouble and much discomfort.

THE CHOLERA

And now that we were fairly on the way the whole atmosphere, so to speak, seemed changed. Instead of the discordant violin and more discordant voices, with the fantastic night open-air dances, with mother earth as a floor, there soon prevailed a more sober mien, even among the young people, as they began to encounter the fatigue of a day's drive and the cares of a night watch. With so many, the watchword was to push ahead and make as big a day's drive as possible, it is not to be wondered at that nearly the whole of the thousand wagons that crossed the river after we did soon passed us.

"Now, fellers, just let 'em rush on, and keep cool, we'll overcatch them afore long," said McAuley. And we did, and passed many a brokendown team, the result of that first few days of rush. It was this class that unloaded such piles of provisions, noted elsewhere, in the first two-hundred-mile stretch, and that fell such easy prey to the ravages of the epidemic of cholera that struck the moving column where the throng from the south side of the Platte began crossing. As I recollect this, it must have been near where the city of Kearney now stands, which is about two hundred miles west of the Missouri river. We had been in the buffalo country several days, and some of our young men had had the keen edge of the hunting zeal worn off by a day's ride in the heat, a number of whom were sick from the effects of overheating and indiscreet drinking of impure water. Such an experience came vividly home to me in the case of my brother Oliver, who had outfitted with our Hoosier friends near Indianapolis, but had crossed the Missouri river in company with us. Being of an adventurous spirit, he could not restrain his ardor, and gave chase to the buffaloes, and fell sick almost unto death. This occurred just at the time when we had encountered the cholera panic, and of course it must be the cholera that had seized him with such an iron grip, argued some of his companions. His old-time comrades and neighbors, all but two, said they could not delay. I said, "It's certain death to take him along in that condition," which they admitted was true. "Divide the outfit, then!" The Davenport brothers said they would not leave my brother, and so their portion of the outfit was put out also, which gave the three a wagon and team. Turning to Buck, I said, "I can't ask you to stay with me." The answer came back quick as a flash, "I am going to stay with you without asking," and he did, too, though my brother was almost a total stranger. We nursed the sick man for four days amidst scenes of excitement and death I hope never to witness again, with the result that on the fifth day we were able to go on and take the convalescent with us and thus saved his life. It was at this point the sixteen hundred wagons passed us as noted elsewhere in the fourdays detention, and loose stock so numerous we made no attempt to count or estimate them.

Of course this incident is of no special importance, except to illustrate what life meant in those strenuous days. The experience of that camp was the experience, I may say, of hundreds of others, of friends parting, of desertion, of noble sacrifice, of where the best and worst of the inner man was shown. Like the dissolving clouds of a brightening summer day, the trains seemed to dissolve and disappear, while no one seemed to know what had become of their component parts, or whither they had gone.

There did seem instances that would convert the most skeptical to the Presbyterian doctrine of total depravity, so brutal and selfish were the actions of some men; brutal to men and women alike; to dumb brutes, and in fact to themselves. And yet alongside of this, it is a pleasure to record that there were numerous instances of noble self-sacrifice, of helpfulness, of unselfishness, to the point of imperiling their own lives. It became a common saying that to *know* one's neighbors, they must be seen on the Plains.

EXTENT OF EMIGRATION

The army of loose stock that accompanied this huge caravan, a column, we may almost say, of five hundred miles long without break, added greatly to the discomfort of all. Of course it will never be known the number of such or for that matter of the emigrants themselves, but their numbers were legion compared to those that labored under the yoke. A conservative estimate would be not less than six animals to the wagon, and surely there were three loose animals to where there was one laboring. By this it would appear that, while there were sixteen hundred wagons passed while we tarried four days, there were nearly ten thousand beasts of burden passed under review, and near thirty thousand loose stock. As to the number of persons, certainly there were five to the wagon, maybe more, but calling it five, eight thousand people, men, women, and children, passed on, many to their graves not afar off.

We know by the inscribed dates found on Independence Rock and elsewhere that there were wagons full three hundred miles ahead of us, and that the throng had continued to pass the river more than a month after we had crossed, so that it does not require a stretch of the imagination to say the column was five hundred miles long, and, like Sherman's march through Georgia, fifty thousand strong.

THE CASUALTIES

Of the casualties in that mighty army I scarcely dare guess. It is certain that history does not give a record of so great a number migrating so long a distance as that of the Pioneers of the Plains, where, as we have seen, the dead lay in rows of fifties and groups of seventies. Shall we say ten per cent fell by the wayside? Many will exclaim that estimate is too low. Ten per cent would give us five thousand sacrifices of lives laid down even in one year to the peopling of the Pacific Coast states. The roll call was never made, and we know not how many there were. The list of mortalities is unknown, and so we are lost in conjecture, and now we know only that the unknown and unmarked graves have gone into oblivion.

CHAPTER V

THE HIGH COURT
LAW OF SELF-PRESERVATION

WHEN WE STEPPED FOOT upon the right bank of the Missouri River we were outside the pale of civil law. We were within the Indian country where no organized civil government existed. Some people and some writers have assumed that each man was a law unto himself and free to do his own will, dependent, of course, upon his physical ability to enforce it.

Nothing could be further from the facts than this assumption, as evil doers soon found out to their discomfiture. No general organization for law and order was effected, but the American instinct for fair play and for a hearing prevailed, so that while there was not mob law, the law of self-preservation asserted itself, and the mandates of the level-headed old men prevailed, "a high court from which there is no appeal," but "a high court in the most exalted sense; a senate composed of the ablest and most respected fathers of the emigration, exercising both legislative and judicial power; and its laws and decisions proved equal and worthy of the high trust reposed in it." So tersely described by Applegate as to conditions when the first great train moved out on the Plains in 1843, that I quote his words as describing conditions in 1852. There was this difference, however, in the emigration of 1843—all, by an agreement, belonged to one or the other of the two companies, the "cow column" or the "light brigade," while with the emigrants of 1852 it is safe to say that more than half did not belong to large companies, or one might say any organized company at all. But this made no difference, for when an occasion called for action a "high court" was convened, and woe betide the man that would undertake to defy its mandates after its deliberations were made public.

CAPITAL PUNISHMENT

One incident, well up on the Sweetwater, will illustrate the spirit and determination of the sturdy old men (elderly I should say, as no young men were allowed to sit in these councils) of the Plains, while laboring under stress of grave personal cares and with many personal bereavements. A murder had been committed, and it was clear the motive was robbery. The suspect had a large family, and was traveling along with the moving column. Men had volunteered to search for the missing man and finally found the proof pointing to the guilty man. A council of twelve men was called and deliberated until the second day, meanwhile holding the murderer safely within their grip. What were they to do? Here was a wife and four little children dependent upon this man for their lives; what would become of this man's family if justice was meted out to him? Soon there came an undercurrent of what might be termed public opinion—that it was probably better to forego punishment than to endanger the lives of the family; but the council would not be swerved from their resolution, and at sundown of the third day the criminal was hung in the presence of the whole camp, including the family, but not until ample provisions had been made to insure the safety of the family by providing a driver to finish the journey. I came so near seeing this that I did see the ends of the wagon tongues in the air and the rope dangling in the air, but I have forgottien the names of the parties, and even if I had not, would be loath to make them public.

From necessity, murder was punishable with death; but stealing, by a tacit understanding, with whipping, which, when inflicted by one of those long ox lashes in the hands of an expert, was a terrible castigation, as the sting of the lash would bring the blood from the victim's back at every stroke. Minor offenses or differences generally took the form of an arbitration, the decision of which each party would abide as if emanating from a court of law.

Lawlessness was not common on the Plains, no more so than in the communities from which the great body of the emigrants had been drawn, and in fact we may safely say not so much, as punishment was swift and certain, and that fact had its deterent effect. But the great body of the emigrants were a law-abiding set from law-abiding communities.

CHAPTER VI

THE OX
THE OX PASSING

THE OX IS PASSING; In fact we may almost say has passed. Like the old-time spinningwheel and the hand loom, that are only to be seen as mementos of the past; or the quaint old cobblers bench with its hand-made lasts and shoe pegs; or the heavy iron bubbling mush pot on the crane in the chimney corner; like the fast vanishing of the old-time men and women of fifty years or more ago—all are passing, to be laid aside for the new ways and the new actors on the scenes of life. While these ways and these scenes and these actors have had their day, yet their experiences and the lessons taught are not lost to the world although at times almost forgotten.

The difference between a civilized and an untutored people lies in the application of these experiences; while the one builds upon the foundations of the past, which engenders hope and ambition for the future, the other has no past nor aspirations for the future. As reverence for the past dies out in the breasts of a generation, so likewise patriotism wanes. In the measure that the love of the history of the past dies, so likewise do the higher aspirations for the future. To keep the flame of patriotism alive we have only to keep the memory of the past vividly in mind.

THE BATTLE OF PEACE

Bearing these thoughts in mind, this expedition to perpetuate the memory of the old Oregon Trail was undertaken. And there was this further thought, that here was this class of heroic men and women who fought a veritable battle—a battle of peace to be sure, yet as brave a battle as any by those that faced the cannon's mouth; a battle that was fraught with as momentous results as any of the great battles of grim war; a battle that wrested half a continent from the native race and from a mighty nation contending for mastery in the unknown regions of the West, whose fame was scantily acknowledged and whose name was already almost forgotten, and whose track, the battle-ground of peace, was on the verge of impending oblivion. Shall this be come an accomplished fact? The answer to this is this expedition, to perpetuate the memory of the old Oregon Trail, and to honor the intrepid pioneers who made it and saved this great region, the old Oregon country, for American rule.

The ox team did it. Had it not been for the patient ox with the wagon train, the preponderance of an American settlement in the old Oregon country over that of the British could not have so certainly prevailed; and in fact uncertainty hovered over the land with results hanging in the balance until that first wagon train reached the region of contending forces.

CHAPTER VII

THE OX TEAM BRIGADE AND THE COW COLUMN EMIGRATION OF 1843

SIXTY-THREE YEARS AGO (1843) a company numbering nearly one thousand strong, of men, women, and children, with over five thousand cattle, guided by such intrepid men as Peter Burnett (afterwards first governor of California), Jesse Applegate, always a first citizen in the community where he had cast his lot, and James W. Nesbitt, afterwards one of the first senators from the state of Oregon, made their way with ox and cow teams toilsomely up the Platte valley, up the Sweetwater, through the South Pass of the Rocky mountains, and across rivers to Fort Hall on the upper waters of Snake river. This far there had been a few traders' wagons and the track had been partially broken for this thousand mile stretch. Not so for the remainder of their journey of near eight hundred miles. Not a wheel had been turned west of this post (then the abiding place for the "watch dogs" of the British, the Hudson Bay Company, who cast a covetous eye upon the great Oregon country), except the Whitman cart, packed a part of the way, but finally stalled at Fort Boise, a few hundred miles to the west.

This great company, encouraged and guided by Whitman,* took their lives in their hands when they cut loose from Fort Hall and headed their teams westward over an almost unexplored region with only

---

*Mrs. N. M. Bogart of Renton, Washington, yet living, who crossed the Plains In 1843, with the cow column of the emigration of that year, recently told the author of a beautiful Incident illustrating the character of the Intrepid missionary, Marcus Whitman, on that memorable trip. "When we came to the crossing of Platte River, some one had to go ahead of the teams to avoid deep holes," she related. "I distinctly remember seeing Whitman take the front yoke of cattle to the front wagon and wade alongside of them. He was stripped of all clothing except his underwear and prepared to swim, If need be, but we all crossed in safety under his guiding hand. He was a great, good man."

Indians' or traders' horseback trails before them and hundreds of miles of mountainous country to traverse.

HORACE GREELEY'S OPINION

"For what," wrote Horace Greeley in his paper, the *New York Tribune*, July 22, 1843, "do they brave the desert, the wilderness, the savage, the snowy precipices of the Rocky Mountains, the weary summer march, the storm-drenched bivouac and the gnawings of famine? This emigration of more than a thousand persons in one body to Oregon wears an aspect of insanity."

The answer came back in due time, "for what" they braved the dangers of a trip across the Plains to an almost unknown land, in petitions praying for help to hold the country they had, as we might say, seized; for recognition as American citizens to be taken under the fostering care of the home government that their effort might not fail. And yet five long years passed and no relief came. An army had been assembled, an Indian war fought, when, at the dying moment of Congress, under the stress of public opinion, aroused by the atrocious massacre of Whitman, party passion on the slavery question was smothered, the long-looked for relief came, and the Oregon bill was passed. They had "held the Fort" till victory perched upon their banner, and the foundation was laid for three great free states to enter the Union.

No more heroic deed is of record than this, to span the remainder of a continent by the wagon track. Failure meant intense suffering to all and death to many. There was no retreat. They had, in a figurative sense, "burned their bridges behind them." Go on they must, or perish.

CAUSE THAT SAVED OREGON FROM BRITISH RULE

When this train safely arrived, the preponderance of the American settlers was so great that there was no more question as to who should temporarily possess the Oregon country. An American provisional government was immediately organized, the British rule was challenged, and Oregon was "saved," and gave three great states to the Union,* and a large part of two more.

---

*Tho first attempt to form an American provisional government only prevailed by one majority and finally fell because of the lack of American preponderance.

Other ox team brigades came. Fourteen hundred people in 1844 followed the track made in 1843, and three thousand in 1845, and on August 15 of that year the Hudson Bay Company accepted the protection of the provisional government and paid taxes to its officers.

Shall we let the memory of such men and women smolder in our minds and sink into oblivion? Shall we refuse to recognize their great courageous acts and fail to do honor to their memory? We erect monuments to commemorate the achievements of grim war and to mark the bloody battlefields; then why shall we not honor those who went out to the battle of the Plains?—a battle of peace, to be sure, yet a battle that called for as heroic deeds and for as great sacrifice as any of war and fraught with as momentous results as the most sanguinary battles of history. The people that held Oregon with such firm grip till the sacrifice came that ended all contention deserve a tender place in the hearts of the citizens of this great commonwealth.

A glimpse into the life of the struggling mass of the first wagon train is both interesting and useful, interesting in the study of social life of the past, and useful from an historical point of view.

JESSE APPLEGATE'S EPIC

Jesse Applegate, leader of the "cow column," after the division into two companies, many years afterwards wrote of the trip, and his account has been published and republished and may be found in full in the Oregon Historical Quarterly. His writing is accepted as classic, and his facts, from first hands, as true to the letter.

Portraying the scenes with the "cow column" for one day he wrote:

> It is 4:00 o'clock A.M.; the sentinels on duty have discharged their rifles—the signal that the hours of sleep are over—and every wagon and tent is pouring forth its night tenants, and slow kindling smokes begin lazily to rise and float away in the morning air. Sixty men start from the corral, spreading as they make through the vast herd of cattle and horses that make a semicircle around the encampment, the most distant perhaps two miles away.
>
> The herders pass the extreme verge and carefully examine for trails beyond to see that none of the animals have strayed or been stolen during the night. This morning no trails lead beyond the outside animals in sight, and by five o'clock the

herders begin to contract the great moving circle, and the well-trained animals move slowly towards camp, clipping here and there a thistle or a tempting bunch of grass on the way. In about an hour five thousand animals are close up to the encampment, and the teamsters are busy selecting their teams and driving them inside the corral to be yoked. The corral is a circle one hundred yards deep formed with wagons connected strongly with each other; the wagon in the rear being connected with the wagon in front by its tongue and ox chains. It is a strong barrier that the most vicious ox can not break, and in case of attack from the Sioux would be no contemptible intrenchment.

From 6:00 to 7:00 o'clock is the busy time; breakfast is to be eaten, the tents struck, the wagons loaded and the teams yoked and brought up in readiness to be attached to their respective wagons. All know when, at 7:00 o'clock, the signal to march sounds, that those not ready to take their places in the line of march must fall into the dusty rear for the day. There are sixty wagons. They have been divided into fifteen divisions or platoons of four wagons each, and each platoon is entitled to lead in its turn. The leading platoon today will be the rear one tomorrow, and will bring up the rear, unless some teamster, through indolence or negligence, has lost his place in the line, and is condemned to that uncomfortable post. It is within ten minutes of 7:00; the corral, but now a strong barricade, is everywhere broken, the teams being attached to the wagons. The women and children have taken their places in them. The pilot (a borderer who has passed his life on the verge of civilization, and has been chosen to his post of leader from his knowledge of the savage and his experience in travel through roadless wastes) stands ready, in the midst of his pioneers and aids, to mount and lead the way. Ten or fifteen young men, not today on duty, form another cluster. They are ready to start on a buffalo hunt, are well mounted and well armed, as they need to be, for the unfriendly Sioux has driven the buffalo out of the Platte, and the hunters must ride fifteen or twenty miles to find them. The cow drivers are hastening, as they get ready, to the rear of their charge, to collect and prepare them for the day's march.

It is on the stroke of 7:00; the rush to and fro, the cracking of whips, the loud command to oxen, and what seemed to be the inextricable confusion of the last ten minutes has ceased. Fortunately every one has been found and every teamster is at his post. The clear notes of a trumpet sound in the front; the pilot and his guards mount their horses; the leading divisions of the wagons move out of the encampment, and take up the line of march; the rest fall into their places with the precision of clock-work, until the spot so lately full of life sinks back into that solitude that seems to reign over the broad plain and rushing river as the caravan draws its lazy length towards the distant El Dorado.

The pilot, by measuring the ground and timing the speed of the horses, has determined the rate of each, so as to enable him to select the nooning place as nearly as the requisite grass and water can be had at the end of five hours' travel of the wagons. Today, the ground being favorable, little time has been lost in preparing the road, so that he and his pioneers are at the nooning place an hour in advance of the wagons, which time is spent in preparing convenient watering places for the animals, and digging little wells near the bank of the Platte. As the teams are not unyoked, but simply turned loose from the wagons, a corral is not formed at noon, but the wagons are drawn up in columns, four abreast, the leading wagon of each platoon on the left, the platoons being formed with that in view. This brings friends together at noon as well as at night.

Today an extra session of the council is being held, to settle a dispute that does not admit of delay, between a proprietor and a young man who has undertaken to do a man's service on the journey for bed and board. Many such cases exist, and much interest is taken in the manner in which this high court, from which there is no appeal, will define the rights of each party in such engagements. The council was a high court in the most exalted sense. It was a senate composed of the ablest and most respected fathers of the emigration. It exercised both legislative and judicial powers, and its laws and decisions proved equal, and worthy of the high trust reposed in it. . . .

It is now one o'clock; the bugle has sounded and the caravan has resumed its westward journey. It is in the same order, but the evening is far less animated than the morning march. A drowsiness has fallen apparently on man and beast; teamsters drop asleep on their perches, and the words of command are now addressed to the slowly creeping oxen in the soft tenor of women or the piping treble of children, while the snores of the teamsters make a droning accompaniment. . . .

The sun is now getting low in the west, and at length the painstaking pilot is standing ready to conduct the train in the circle which he has previously measured and marked out, which is to form the invariable fortification for the night. The leading wagons follow him so nearly around the circle that but a wagon length separates them. Each wagon follows in its track, the rear closing on the front, until its tongue and ox chains will perfectly reach from one to the other; and so accurate [is] the measure and perfect the practice that the hindmost wagon of the train always precisely closes the gateway. As each wagon is brought into position it is dropped from the team (the teams being inside the circle), the team is unyoked, and the yoke and chains are used to connect the wagon strongly with that in its front. Within ten minutes from the time the leading wagon halted, the barricade is formed, the teams unyoked and driven out to pasture. Everyone is busy preparing fires . . . to cook the evening meal, pitching tents and otherwise preparing for the night

The watches begin at 8:00 o'clock P.M. and end at 4:00 A.M.

CHAPTER VIII

LIFE ON THE PLAINS
OPENING THE ROAD

THE READER WILL NOTE, "To-day, the ground being favorable, little time has been lost in preparing the road," showing the arduous task before them in road making. The search for the best route to avoid steep pitches or rocky points or high sage brush required constant vigilance on the part of the "pioneers" whose duty, with the pilot, was to spy out and prepare the way for the caravan to follow. At the noon hour, I note, "As the teams are not unyoked, but simply turned loose from the wagon, a corral is not formed," a cruel practice I frequently saw in 1852. It is with pride I can write that neither Buck and Dandy in 1852, nor Twist and Dave in 1906, ever stood with the yoke on while I lunched, and that the former were in better condition when the trip was ended than when they started, even though they were at the start unbroken steers. Twist and Dave have come through the ordeal in as good condition as at the start, until Twist was poisoned and died, although they alone have brought the one wagon (weighing 1,400 pounds) and its load all the way, a distance of nearly 1,700 miles.

A word as to the rules of the expedition just completed. Long before the summer solstice, the alarm clock was set at 4:00, breakfast over by 5:00, and the start usually made by 6:00 o'clock. We always took a long nooning hour, and if warm, several hours, and then traveled late, making from fifteen to twenty-five miles a day, averaging seventeen and a half miles for traveling days. Slow, you will say. Yes; slow but sure.

MODE OF TRAVEL IN 1852

And now as to our mode of travel in 1852. I did not enter an organized company, neither could I travel alone. Four wagons, with nine men, by a tacit agreement, traveled together for a thousand miles, and separated only when our roads parted, the one to California and the other to Oregon. And yet we were all the while in one great train, never out of the sight or hearing of others. In fact, at times the road would be so full of wagons that all could not travel in one track, and this fact accounts for the double road beds seen in so many places on the trail. One of the party always went ahead to look out for water, grass, and fuel, three requisites for a camping place. The grass along the beaten track was always eaten off close by the loose stock, of which there were great numbers, and so we had frequently to take the cattle long distances. Then came the most trying part of the whole trip—the all-night watch, which resulted in our making the cattle our bedfellows, back to back for warmth; for signal as well, to get up if the ox did. It was not long though till we were used to it, and slept quite a bit except when a storm struck us; well, then it was, to say the least, not a pleasure outing. But weren't we glad when the morning came, and perchance the smoke of the campfire might be in sight, and maybe, as we approached, we could catch the aroma of the coffee. And then such tender greetings and such thoughtful care that would have touched a heart of stone, and to us seemed like a paradise. We were supremely happy.

ABANDONED PROPERTY

People too often brought their own ills upon themselves by their indiscreet action, especially in the loss of their teams. The trip had not progressed far till there came a universal outcry against the heavy loads and unnecessary articles, and soon we begun to see abandoned property. First it might be a table or a cupboard or perchance a bedstead or a heavy cast-iron, cookstove. Then began to be seen bedding by the wayside, feather beds, blankets, quilts, pillows, everything of the kind that mortal man might want. Not so very long till here and there an abandoned wagon was to be seen, provisions, stacks of flour, and bacon being the most abundant, all left as common property. Help yourself if you will, no one will interfere, and in fact in some places a sign was posted inviting all to take what they wanted. Hundreds of wagons were left and hundreds of tons of goods. People seemed to vie with each other to give away their property, there being no chance to sell, and they disliked to destroy. Long after the mania for getting rid of goods and lightening the load the abandonment of wagons continued, as the teams became weaker (generally from abuse or lack of care), and the ravages of cholera struck us. It was then that many lost their heads and ruined their teams by furious driving, by lack of care, and by abuse. There came a veritable stampede, a strife for possession of the road, to see who should get ahead. Whole trains with bad blood would strive for mastery of the road, one attempting to pass the other, frequently with drivers on each side the team to urge the poor, suffering dumb brutes forward.

THE CHOLERA

"What shall we do?" passed from one to another in our little family council.

"Now, fellers," said McAuley, "don't lose your heads, but do just as you have been doing; you gals, just make your bread as light as ever, and we'll boil the water and take river water the same as ever, even if it is almost thick as mud."

We had all along refused to "dig little wells near the bank of the Platte," as noted by Applegate in his quoted article, having soon learned that the water obtained was strongly charged with alkali, while the river water was comparatively pure other than the fine impalpable sand, so fine, one might almost say, as to be held in solution.

"Keep cool," he continued; "maybe we'll have to lay down, and maybe not. Anyway, it's no use a frettin'. What's to be will be, specially if we but help things along."

This homely wise counsel fell upon willing ears, as most all were already of the same mind, and we did, "just as we had been doing," and escaped unharmed.

I look back on that party of nine men and three women (and a baby) with four wagons with feelings almost akin to reverence.

Thomas McAuley became by natural selection the leader of the party although no agreement of the kind was ever made. He was, next to his maiden sister, the oldest of the party, a most fearless man and never "lost his head," whatever the emergency might arise, and I have been in some pretty tight places with him. While he was the oldest, I was the youngest of the men folks of the party, and the only married man of the lot, and if I do have to say it myself, the strongest and ablest to bear the brunt of the work (pardon me, reader, when I add and willing according to my strength, for it is true), and so we got along well together till the parting of the way came. This spirit, though, pervaded the whole camp both with the men and women folks to the end. Thomas McAuley still lives, at Hobart Mills, California, or did but a couple of years ago when I last heard from him, a respected citizen. He has long ago passed the eighty-year mark, and has not "laid down" yet.

THE HAPPY FAMILY

Did space but permit I would like to tell more in detail of the members of that little happy party (family we called ourselves), camped near the bank of the Platte when the fury of that great epidemic burst upon us, but I can only make brief mention. William Buck, my partner, a noble man, has long ago "laid down." Always scrupulously neat and cleanly, always ready to cater to the wants of his companions and as honest as the day is long, he has ever held a tender place in my heart. It was Buck that selected our nice little outfit complete in every part, so that we did not throw away a pound of provisions nor need to purchase any. The water can was in the wagon, of sufficient capacity to supply our wants for a day, and a "sup" for the oxen and cows besides. The milk can stood near by and always yielded up its lump of butter at nght, churned by the movement of the wagon from the surplus morning's milk. The yeast cake so thoughtfully provided by the little wife ever brought forth sweet, light bread baked in that tin reflector before the "chip" (buffalo) fire. That reflector and those yeast cakes were a great factor conducive to our health. Small things, to be sure, but great as to results. Instead of saleratus biscuit, bacon, and beans we had the light bread and fruit with fresh meats and rice pudding far out on the Plains, until our supply of eggs became exhausted.

Of the remainder of the party, brother Oliver "laid down" forty-five years ago, but his memory is still green in the hearts of all who knew him. Margaret McAuley died a few years after reaching California. Like her brother, she was resolute and resourceful and almost like a mother to the younger sister and the young little wife and baby. And such a baby! If one were to judge by the actions of all members of that camp, the conclusion would be reached there was no other such on earth. All seemed rejoiced to know there was a baby in camp—young (only seven weeks old when we started), but strong and grew apace as the higher altitude was reached.

Eliza, the younger sister, a type of the healthy, handsome American girl, graceful and modest, became the center of attraction upon which a romance might be written, but as the good elderly ladj still lives, the time has not yet come, and so we must draw the veil.

Of the two Davenport brothers, Jacob, the youngest, took sick at Soda Springs, was confined to the wagon for more than eight hundred miles down Snake River in that intolerable dust, and finally died soon after we arrived in Portland.

John, the elder brother, always fretful, but willing to do his part, has passed out of my knowledge. Both came of respected parents on an adjoining farm to that of my own home near Indianapolis, but I have lost all trace of them.

Perhaps the general reader may not take even a passing interest in this little party (family) here described. I can only say that this was typical of many such on the Trail of '52. The McAuleys or Buck and others of our party could be duplicated in larger or smaller parties all along the line. There were hundreds of noble men trudging up the Platte at that time in an army over five hundred miles long, many of whom "laid down," a sacrifice to duty, or maybe to inherent weakness of their systems. While it is true such an experience brings out the worst features of individual characters, yet it is nevertheless true the shining virtues come to the front likewise; like pure gold, is often found where least expected.

HEROIC PIONEER WOMAN

Of the fortitude of the women one can not say too much. Embarrassed at the start by the follies of fashion (and long dresses which were quickly discarded and the bloomer donned), they soon rose to the occasion and cast false modesty aside. Could we but have had the camera (of course not then in existence) on one of those typical camps, what a picture there would be. Elderly matrons dressed almost as like the little sprite miss of tender years of to-day. The younger women more shy of accepting the inevitable, but finally fell into the procession, and we had a community of women wearing bloomers without invidious comment, or in fact of any comment at all. Some of them soon went barefoot, partly from choice and in other cases from necessity. The same could be said of the men, as shoe leather began to grind out from the sand and dry heat. Of all the fantastic costumes it is safe to say the like before was never seen nor equaled. The scene beggars description. Patches became visible upon the clothing of preachers as well as laymen; the situation brooked no respect of persons. The grandmother's cap was soon displaced by a handkerchief or perhaps a bit of cloth. Grandfather's high crowned hat disappeared as if by magic. Hatless and bootless men became a common sight. Bonnetless women were to be seen on all sides. They wore what they had left or could get without question of the fitness of things. Rich dresses were worn by some ladies because they had no others left; the gentlemen drew on their wardrobes till scarcely a fine unsoiled suit was left.

HARDSHIPS

The dust has been spoken of as intolerable. The word hardly expresses the situation; in fact, I can not say the English language contains the word to define it. Here was a moving mass of humanity and dumb brutes at times mixed in inextricable confusion a hundred feet wide or more. At times two columns of wagons traveling on parallel lines and near each other served as a barrier to prevent loose stock from crossing, but usually there would be an almost inextricable mass of cows, young cattle, horses, and footmen moving along the outskirts. Here and there would be the drivers of loose stock, some on foot and some on horseback; a young girl maybe riding astride with a younger child behind, going here and there after an intractible cow, while the mother could be seen in the confusion lending a helping hand. As in a thronged city street, no one seemed to look to the right or to the left, or pay much if any attention to others, bent alone on accomplishment of their task in hand. Over all, in calm weather at times the dust would settle so thick that the lead team of oxen could not be seen from the wagon; like a London fog, so thick one might almost cut it.* Then again, that steady flow of wind up to and through the South Pass would hurl the dust and sand in one's face sometimes with force enough to sting from the impact upon the face and hands.

Then we had storms that were not of sand and wind alone; storms that only a Platte valley in summer or a Puget Sound winter might turn out; storms that would wet to the skin in less time than it takes to write this sentence. One such I remember being caught in while out on watch. The cattle traveled so fast it was difficult to keep up with them. I could do nothing else than follow, as it would have been as impossible to turn them as it would have been to change the direction of the wind. I have always thought of this as a cloudburst. Anyway, there was not a dry thread left on me in an incredibly short time. My boots were as full of water as if I had been wading over boot-top deep, and the water ran through my hat as if it had been a sieve, almost blinding me in the fury of wind and water. Many tents were leveled, and in fact such occurrences as fallen tents were not uncommon. One of our neighboring trains suffered no inconsiderable loss by the sheets of water on the ground, floating their

*The author spent four winters in London on the world's hop market, and perhaps has a more vivid recollection of what is meant by a London fog than would be understood by the general reader. I have seen the fog and smoke there so black that one could not see his hand held at arm's length, and it reminded me of some of the scenes of the dust on the Plains.

camp equipage, ox yokes, and all loose articles away; and they only narrowly escaped having a wagon engulfed in the raging torrent that came so unexpectedly upon them. Such were some of the discomforts on the Plains in '52.

On my 1906 trip I have encountered very little dust. In the early part of it we had some furious rains, considerable snow, and a little hail, but we had no watches to make, no stock to follow, no fear but that Twist and Dave would be easily found when morning came. These faithful oxen soon came to know the hand that fed them, and almost invariably would come to the wagon at nightfall for their nose bags of rolled oats or cracked corn. Nevertheless, the trip has not been entirely a picnic and entirely devoid of cares and fatigue. Too much of a good thing, it is said, spoils the whole. And so it is with travel day in and day out, from week to week, month to month, till the year is half gone. It is, to say the least, "wearin'," using an old-time western phrase the reader will understand, whether he ever heard it before or not. But to my friends who would have it that I was to encounter untold hardships; that I was "going out on the Plains to die"; that I would never get back alive—I conjure such to sleep soundly and not let the hardships bother them, for I have not yet met my sick day for the fifty-four years since passing this great river, the Missouri. And now let us take up the thread of particulars of our journey westward.

CHAPTER IX

RIVER CROSSINGS
WAGON BEDS AS BOATS

IN 1852 THERE WERE BUT FEW FERRIES and none in many places where crossings were to be made, and where here and there a ferry was found the charges were high, or perhaps the word should be exorbitant, and out of reach of a large majority of the emigrants. In my own case, all my funds had been absorbed in procuring my outfit at Eddyville, Iowa, not dreaming there would be use for money "on the Plains," where there were neither supplies nor people. We soon found out our mistake, however, and became watchful to mend matters when opportunity offered. The crossing of Snake River, though late in the trip, gave the opportunity.

About thirty miles below Salmon Falls the dilemma confronted us to either cross the river or let our teams starve on the trip down the river on the south bank. Some trains had caulked three wagon-beds and lashed them together and were crossing, and would not help others across for less than three to five dollars a wagon, the party swimming their own stock. If others could cross in wagon-beds, why could I not do so likewise? and without much ado all the old clothing that could possibly be spared was marshaled, tar buckets ransacked, old chisels and broken knives hunted up, and a veritable boat repairing and caulking campaign inaugurated; and shortly the wagon box rode placidly, even if not gracefully on the turbid waters of the formidable river. It had been my fortune to be the strongest physically of any of our little party of four men, though I would cheerfully accept a second place mentally.

My boyhood pranks of playing and paddling logs or old leaky skiffs in the waters of White River now served me well, for I could row a boat even if I had never taken lessons as an athlete. My first venture across Snake River was with the whole of the wagon gear run over the wagon box, the whole being gradually worked out into deep water. The load was so heavy that a very small margin was left to prevent the water from breaking over the sides, and some actually did as light ripples on the surface struck the "Mary Jane," as we had christened (without wine) the "craft" as she was launched. But I got over safely; yet after that took lighter loads and really enjoyed the novelty of the work and the change from the intolerable dust to the atmosphere of the water.

DOWN SNAKE RIVER IN WAGON BOXES

Some were so infatuated with the idea of floating on the water as to be easily persuaded by an unprincipled trader at the lower crossing to dispose of their teams for a song, and embark in their wagon beds for a voyage down the river. It is needless to say that all such (of which there were a goodly number) lost everything they had and some their lives, the survivors, after incredible hardships, reaching the road again to become objects of charity where separated entirely from friends. I knew one survivor, who yet lives in our state, that was out seven days without food other than a scant supply of berries and vegetable growth, and "a few crickets, but not many," as it was too laborious to catch them.

We had no trouble to cross the cattle, although the river was wide. Dandy would do almost anything I asked of him, so, leading him to the water's edge, with a little coaxing I got him into swimming water and guided him across with the wagon bed, while the others all followed, having been driven into the deep water following the leader. It seems almost incredible how passively obedient cattle will become after long training on such a trip in crossing streams.

We had not finished crossing when tempting offers came from others to cross them, but all of our party said "No, we must travel." The rule had been adopted to travel some every day possible. Travel, travel, travel, was the watchword, and nothing would divert us from that resolution, and so on the third day we were ready to pull out from the river with the cattle rested from the enforced detention.

But what about the lower crossing? Those who had crossed over the river must somehow or another get back. It was less than 150 miles to where we were again to cross back to the south side (left bank) of the river. I could walk that in three days, while it would take our teams ten. Could I not go ahead, procure a wagon-box and start a ferry of my own? The thought prompted an affirmative answer at once; so with a little food and a small blanket the trip to the lower crossing was made. It may be ludicrous, but is true, that the most I remember about that trip is the jack rabbits—such swarms of them I had never seen before as I traveled down the Boise valley, and never expect to see the like again. The trip was made in safety, but conditions were different. At the lower crossing, as I have already said, some were disposing of their teams and starting to float down the river; some were fording, a perilous undertaking, but most of them succeeded who tried, and besides a trader whose name I have forgotten had an established ferry near the old fort (Boise). But I soon obtained the wagon-bed and was at work during all of the daylight hours (no eight-hour-a-day there) crossing people till the teams came up, and for several days after, and left the river with $110 in my pocket, all of which was gone before I arrived in Portland, save $12.75.

I did not look upon that work then other than as a part of the trip to do the best we could. None of us thought we were doing a heroic act in crossing the plains and meeting emergencies as they arose. In fact, we did not think at all of that phase of the question. Many have, however, in later life looked upon their achievements with pardonable pride, and some in a vain-glorious mood of mind.

CHAPTER X

RAVAGES OF THE CHOLERA

TO MANY THE STRAIN upon the system was great and suffering intense, and to such small wonder if the recollections are a little colored in their minds. For myself, I can truly say that in after pioneer life on Puget Sound there was as great discomfort as on the Plains, but neither experience laid a firm grip upon me, as may be testified by the fact that in all that experience, on the Plains, and since, to the day of this writing never have I been a day sick in bed. But I saw much suffering and the loss of life from the ravages of cholera was appalling. L. B. Rowland, now of Engen, Oregon, recently told me of the experience of his train of twenty-three persons, between the two crossings of Snake River, of which we have just written. Of the twenty-three that crossed eleven died before they reached the lower crossing. Other trains suffered, but probably few to such a great extent. But all down the Snake the dust and heat were great. They were intolerable to many who gave way in despair and died. The little young wife, the companion now of so many years since, soon after took sick and had to be carried in arms up the bank of the Willamette and to the lodging house in Portland, an easy task for me, as the weight incident to health was gone and the frame only left.

THE GREAT PANIC

The scourge of cholera on the Platte in 1852 is far beyond my power of description. In later years I have witnessed panics on shipboard; have experienced the horrors of the flight of a whole population from the grasp of the Indians, but never before nor since such scenes as those in the thickest of the ravages of cholera. It did seem that people lost all control of themselves and of others. Whole trains could be seen contending for the mastery of the road by day, and the power of endurance tested to the utmost both men and beast at night. The scourge came from the south, as we met the trains that crossed the Platte and congested the Trail, one might almost say, both day and night. And small wonder when such scenes occurred as is related. Mrs. M. E. Jones, now of North Yakima, relates that forty people of their train died in one day and two nights before reaching the crossing of the Platte. Martin Cook of Newbury, Oregon, is my authority for the following: A family of seven persons, the father known as "Dad Priels," from Hartford, Warren county, Iowa, all died of cholera and were buried in one grave. He could not tell me the locality nor the exact date, but it would be useless to search for the graves, as all such have long ago been leveled by the passing of the hoofs of the buffalo or domestic stock, or met the fate of hundreds of shallow graves, desecrated by the hungry wolves. While camped with a sick brother four days a short distance above Grand Island, by actual count of one day and estimate for three, sixteen hundred wagons passed by, and a neighboring burial place grew from a few to fifty-two fresh graves.

CHAPTER XI

THE OX TEAM MONUMENT EXPEDITION

TO PERPETUATE THE IDENTITY of the Trail made by the early sturdy pioneers, the battle-ground of peace, to honor the memories of these true heroes and to kindle in the breasts of the rising generation a flame of patriotic sentiment, this expedition was undertaken.

The ox team was chosen as a typical reminder of pioneer days, an effective instrument to attract attention, arouse enthusiasm, and a help to secure aid to forward the work of marking the old Trail, and erecting monuments in centers of population.

In one respect the object was attained, that of attracting attention, with results in part wholly unexpected. I had hardly driven the outfit out of my dooryard till the work of defacing the wagon and wagon cover, and even the nice map of the old Trail began. First I noticed a name or two written on the wagon-bed, then a dozen or more, all stealthily placed there, until the whole was so closely covered there was no room for more. Finally the vandals began carving initials on the bed, cutting off pieces to carry away, until I finally put a stop to it by employing a special police, posting notices, and nabbing some in the very act.

Give me Indians on the Plains to contend with, give me fleas, ah, yes, the detested sage brush ticks to burrow in your flesh, but deliver me from the degenerates of cheap notoriety seekers.

Many good people have thought there was some organization behind this work, or that there had been government aid secured. To all such and to those who may read these lines I will quote from the cards issued at the outset:

> The expense of this expedition to perpetuate the memory of the old Oregon Trail, by erecting stone monuments, is borne by myself except such voluntary aid as may be given by those taking an interest in the work, and you are respectfully solicited to contribute such sum as may be convenient.

To this appeal a generous response has been made, as attested by the line of monuments from Puget Sound to this point a brief account of which, with incidents of this trip and of the trip made by me with an ox and cow team in 1852, will follow.

THE TEAM

The team cousists of one seven-year-old ox, Twist, and one unbroken range four-year-old steer, Dave. When we were ready to start, Twist weighed 1,470 and Dave 1,560 pounds, respectively. This order of weight was soon changed. In three months' time Twist gained 130 and Dave lost 10 pounds. All this time I fed with a lavish hand all the rolled barley I dare and all the hay they would eat. During that time thirty-three days lapsed in which we did not travel, being engaged either arranging for the erection or dedication of monuments.

TEAM OF 1852

My team of 1852 consisted of two unbroken steers and two cows. The cows I had to give up to save the life of the oxen during the deep snow that fell in the winter of 1852-53. The oxen hauled our belongings over to the head of Puget Sound in July, 1853, and I there parted with them. Of that parting I quote from my work *Pioneer Reminiscences of Puget Sound*:

> What I am now about to write may provoke a smile, but I can only say, reader, put yourself in my place. That there should be a feeling akin to affection between a man and an ox will seem past comprehension to many. The time had come when Buck and Dandy and I must part for good and all. I could not transport them to our island home, neither provide for them. These patient, dumb brutes had been my close companions for the long, weary months on the Plains, and had never failed me; they would do my bidding to the letter. I often said Buck understood English better than some people I had seen in my lifetime. I had done what not one in a hundred did; that was to start on that trip with an unbroken ox and cow team. I had selected these four-year-old steers for their intelligent eyes as well as for their trim build, and had made no mistake. We had bivouacked together; actually slept together; lunched together. They knew me as far as they could see, and seemed delighted to obey my word, and I did regret to

feel constrained to part with them. I knew they had assured my safe transit on the weary journey, if not even to the point of having saved my life. I could pack them, ride them, drive them by the word and receive their salutations, and why should I be ashamed to part with feelings of more than regret?

THE OLD OREGON TRAIL 87

I have no such feelings for the brute Twist, for on April 12 he kicked me, almost broke my knee, and came near disabling me for life, and Dave is worse, for they both kick like government mules. If the reader happens to know how that is he will appreciate the definition. Twist, however, is the best all round ox I ever saw. Dave has not yet lost his range spirit entirely, and sometimes gets mad and unruly.

THE WAGON

The wagon is new woodwork throughout except one hub, which did service across the Plains in 1853. The hub bands, boxes, and other irons are from two old-time wagons that crossed the Plains in 1853, and differ some in size and shape; hence the fore and hind wheel hubs do not match. The axles are wood, with the old-time linch pins and steel skeins, involving the use of tar and the tar bucket. The bed is of the old style "prairie schooner" so-called fashioned as a boat, like those of "ye olden times." I crossed Snake River in two places in 1852, with all I possessed (except the oxen and cows), including the running-gear of the wagon, in a wagon-box not as good as this one shown in the illustration.

CAMP NO. 1

Camp No. 1 was in my own front dooryard at Puyallup; Washington, a town established on my own homestead nearly forty years ago, on the line of the Northern Pacific railroad, nine miles southeast of Tacoma, and thirty miles south of Seattle, Washington. In platting the town I dedicated a park and called it Pioneer Park, and in it are the remains of our old ivy-covered cabin, where the wife of fifty-five years ago and I, with our growing family, spent so many happy hours. In this same town I named the principal thoroughfare Pioneer Avenue, and a short street abutting the park Pioneer Way, hence the reader may note it is not a new idea with me to perpetuate the memory of the pioneers.

THE CAMP AT HOME

No piece of machinery ever runs at the start as well as after trial; therefore Camp No. 1 was maintained several days to mend up the weak points, and so after a few days of trial everything was pronounced in order, and Camp No. 2 was pitched in the street in front of the Methodist church of the town, and a lecture delivered in the church for the benefit of the expedition.

TUMWATER, WASHINGTON

The final start was made from Camp No. 9 at Olympia, Washington, the capital of the state of Washington, February 19, 1906, and but two miles from the end of the old Trail—in early days of Oregon but now Washington. The drive to Tumwater was made, a post set at the end of the Trail, and subsequently arrangements completed to substitute an inscribed stone.

TENINO MONUMENT

At Tenino the citizens had prepared and inscribed a suitable stone, and on February 21 the same was dedicated with due ceremony, with nearly the whole population in attendance.

CENTRALIA, WASHINGTON

At Centralia contributions were made sufficient to warrant ordering an inscribed stone, which was done, and in due time was placed in position at the intersection of the Trail and road a short way out from the city.

CHEHALIS, WASHINGTON

At Chehalis a point was selected in the center of the street at the park, and a post set to mark the spot where the monument is to stand. The commercial club undertook the work, but were not ready to erect and dedicate, as a more expensive monument than one that could be speedily obtained would be provided as an ornament to the park.

I very vividly recollected this section of the old Trail, having, in company with a brother, packed my blankets and "grub" on my back over it in May, 1853, and camped on it near by over night, under the sheltering, drooping branches of a friendly cedar tree. We did not carry tents on such a trip, but slept out under the open canopy of heaven, obtaining such shelter as we could from day to day.

CLAQUATO, WASHINGTON

It is permissible to note the liberality of H. C Davis of Claquato, who provided a fund of $50 to erect a monument at Claquato and $50 for the purchase of one ox for the expedition.

JACKSONS

John R. Jackson was the first American citizen to settle north of the Columbia river. One of the daughters, Mrs. Ware, accompanied by her husband, indicated the spot where the monument should be erected, and a post was planted. A touching incident occurred when Mrs. Ware was requested to put the post in place and hold it while her husband tamped the earth around it, which she did with tears streaming from her eyes at the thought that at last her pioneer father's place in history was to be recognized. A stone was ordered at once, to soon take the place of the post.

TOLEDO, WASHINGTON

This village, the last place to reach on the old Trail in Washington, is on the Cowlitz, a mile from the landing where the pioneers left the river for the overland trail to the Sound.

To this point in July, 1853, I shipped my scant belongings from the Columbia river, my wife going up in the same canoe, while I drove Buck and Dandy up the trail on the left bank of the river. A post was planted here on the Trail, and a promise made that a stone monument should soon replace it.

PORTLAND, OREGON

From Toledo I shipped by river steamer the whole outfit, and took passage with my assistants to Portland, thus reversing the order of travel In 1853, accepting the use of steam instead of the brawn of the arm of stalwart men and Indians to propel the canoe, and arrived on the evening of March 1, and on the morning of March 2 pitched our camp in the heart of the city on a beautiful block, the property of Jacob Kamm. I remained in camp here until the morning of March 9, to test the question of securing aid for the expedition.

Very different was the experience when, on October 1, 1852, I carried my sick wife in my arms up the bank of the Willamette River three blocks away to a colored man's lodging house in Portland, with but $2.75 in my pocket and no resource but my labor.

Except for the efforts of that indefatigable worker, George H. Himes, assistant secretary of the Oregon Historical Society, with headquarters in Portland, no helping hand was extended. Not but that the citizens took a lively interest in the "novel undertaking," in this "unique outfit," yet the fact became evident that only the few believed the work could be successfully done by individual effort, and that government aid should be invoked. The prevailing opinion was voiced by a prominent citizen, a trustee of a church, who voted against allowing the use of the church for a lecture for the benefit of the expedition, when he said that he "did not want to do anything to encourage that old man to go out on the Plains to die." Notwithstanding this sentiment, through Mr. Himes's efforts nearly $200 was contributed.

March 10, in early morning hours, embarked at Portland on the steamer *Baily Gatzert*, for The Dalles, which place was reached after night, but enlivened by a warm reception from the citizens awaiting our arrival, who conducted us to a camping place that had been selected.

Upon this steamer one can enjoy all the luxuries of civilized life, a continuous trip now being made through the government locks at the cascades. The tables are supplied with delicacies the season affords, with clean linen for the beds, and obsequious attendants to supply the wants of the travelers.

"What changes time has wrought," I exclaimed. "Can this be the same Columbia River which I traversed fifty-four years ago? Yes, there are the mighty mountains, the wonderful waterfalls, the sunken forests, each attesting the identity of the spot; but what about the conditions?" Reader, pardon me if I make a digression and quote from my reminiscences an account of that trip fifty-four years ago.

CHAPTER XII

FLOATING DOWN THE RIVER*

ON A SEPTEMBER DAY OF 1852 an assemblage of persons could be seen encamped on the banks of the great Columbia, at The Dalles, now a city of no small pretensions, but then only a name for the peculiar configuration of country adjacent to and including the waters of the great river. One would soon discover this assemblage was constantly changing. Every few hours stragglers came in from off the dusty road, begrimed with the sweat of the brow commingled with particles of dust driven through the air, sometimes by a gentle breeze, and then again by a violent gale sweeping up the river through the mountain gap of the Cascade range. A motley crowd these people were, almost cosmopolitan in nationality, yet all vestige of race peculiarities or race prejudices ground away in the mill of adversity and trials common to all alike in common danger. And yet, the dress and appearance of this assemblage were as varied as the human countenance and as unique as the great mountain scenery before them. Some were clad in scanty attire as soiled with the dust as their brows; others, while with better pretensions, lacked some portions of dress required in civilized life. Here a matronly dame with clean apparel would be without shoes, or there, perhaps, the husband without the hat or perhaps both shoes and hat absent; there the youngsters of all ages, making no pretensions to genteel clothing other than to cover their nakedness. An expert's ingenuity would be taxed to the utmost to discover either the texture or original color of the clothing of either juvenile or adult, so prevailing was the patchwork and so inground the particles of dust and sand from off the Plains.

---

*From *Pioneer Reminiscences of Puget Sound, The Tragedy of Leschi* by Ezra Meeker, published and sold by the author. 6x9, 600 pages, cloth $3.00; leather $4.00, Puyallup, Washington.

Some of these people were buoyant and hopeful in the anticipation of meeting friends whom they knew were awaiting them at their journey's end, while others were downcast and despondent as their thoughts went back to their old homes left behind, and the struggle now so near ended, and forward to tlie (to them) unknown land ahead. Some had laid friends and relatives tenderly away in the shifting sands, who had fallen by the wayside, with the certain knowledge that with many the spot selected by them would not be the last resting place for the bones of the loved ones. The hunger of the wolf had been appeased by the abundance of food from the fallen cattle that lined the trail for a thousand miles or more, or from the weakened beasts of the emigrants that constantly submitted to capture by the relentless native animals. Not so for the future, when this supply of food had disappeared.

The story of the trip across the Plains in 1852 is both interesting and pathetic, but I have planned to write of life after the journey rather than much about the journey itself; of the trials that beset the people after their five months' struggle on the tented field of two thousand miles of marching was ended, where, like on the very battlefield, the dead lay in rows of fifties or more; where the trail became so lined with fallen animals one could scarcely be out of sight or smell of carrion; where the sick had no respite from suffering nor the well from fatigue. But this ofttold story is a subject of itself, treated briefiy to the end we may have space to tell what happened when the journey was ended.

The constant gathering on the bank of the Columbia and constant departures of the emigrants did not materially change the numbers encamped, nor the general appearance. The great trip had moulded this army of home-seekers into one homogenous mass, a common brotherhood, that left a lasting impression upon the participants, and, although few are left now, not one but will greet an old comrade as a brother indeed, and, in fact, with hearty and oftentimes tearful congratulations.

We camped but two days on the bank of the river. When I say "we" let it be understood that I mean myself, my young wife, and the little baby boy, who was but seven weeks old when the start was made from near Eddyville, Iowa. Both were sick, the mother from gradual exhaustion during the trip incident to motherhood, and the little one in sympathy, doubtless drawn from the mother's breast.

Did you ever think of the wonderful mystery of the inner action of the mind, how some impressions once made seem to remain, while others gradually fade away, like the twilight of a summer sunset, until iiually lost? And then how seemingly trivial incidents will be fastened upon one's memory while others of more importance we would recall if we could, but which have faded forever from our grasp? I can well believe all readers have had this experience, and so will be prepared to receive with leniency the confession of an elderly gentleman (I will not say old), when he says that most of the incidents are forgotten and few remembered. I do not remember the embarking on the great scow for the float down the river to the Cascades, but vividly remember, as though it were but yesterday, incidents of the voyage. We all felt (I now mean the emigrants who took passage) that now our journey was ended. The cattle had been unyoked for the last time; the wagons had been rolled to the last bivouac; the embers of the last campfire had died out; the last word of gossip had been spoken, and now, we were entering a new field with new present experience, and with new expectancy for the morrow.

The scow or lighter upon which we took passage was decked over, but without railing, a simple, smooth surface upon which to pile our belongings, which, in the great majority of cases made but a very small showing. I think there must have been a dozen families, or more, of sixty or more persons, principally women and children, as the young men (and some old ones, too) were struggling on the mountain trail to get the teams through to the west side. The whole deck surface of the scow was covered with the remnants of the emigrants' outfits, which in turn were covered by the owners, either sitting or reclining upon their possessions, leaving but scant room to change position or move about in any way.

Did you ever, reader, have the experience when some sorrow overtook you, or when some disappointment had been experienced, or when deferred hopes had not been realized, or sometimes even without these and from some unknown, subtle cause, feel that depression of spirits that for lack of a better name we call "the blues?" When the world ahead looked dark; when hope seemed extinguished and the future looked like a blank? Why do I ask this question? I know you all to a greater or less degree have had just this experience. Can you wonder that, after our craft had been turned loose upon the waters of the great river, and begun floating lazily down with the current, that such a feeling as tliat described would seize us as with an iron grip? We were like an army that had burned the bridges behind them as they marched, and with scant knowledge of what lay in the track before them. Here we were, more than two thousand miles from home, separated by a trackless, uninhabited waste of country, impossible for us to retrace our steps. Go ahead we must, no matter what we were to encounter. Then, too, the system had been strung up for months to duties that could not be avoided or delayed, until many were on the verge of collapse. Some were sick and all reduced in flesh from the urgent call for camp duty, and lack of variety of food. Such were the feelings of the motley crowd of sixty persons as we slowly neared that wonderful crevice through which the great river flows while passing the Cascade Mountain range.

For myself, I can truly say that the trip had not drawn on my vitality as I saw with so many. True, I had been worked down in flesh, having lost nearly twenty pounds on the trip, but what weight I had left was the bone and sinew of my system, that served me so well on this trip and has been my comfort in other walks of life at a later period. And so, if asked, did you experience hardship on the trip across the Plains, I could not answer yes without a mental reservation that it might have been a great deal worse. I say the same as to after experience, for these subsequent fifty years or more of pioneer life, having been blessed with a good constitution, and being now able to say that in the fifty-three years of our married life the wife has never seen me a day sick in bed. But this is a digression and so we must turn our attention to the trip on the scow, "floating down the river."

In our company, a party of three, a young married couple and an unmarried sister lounged on their belongings, listlessly watching the ripples on the water, as did also others of the party. But little conversation was passing. Each seemed to be communing with himself or herself, but it was easy to see what were the thoughts occupying the minds of all. The young husband, it was plain to be seen, would soon complete that greater journey to the unknown beyond, a condition that weighed so heavily upon the ladies of the party that they could ill conceal their solicitude and sorrow. Finally, to cheer up the sick husband and brother, the ladies began in sweet subdued voices to sing the old familiar song of "Home, Sweet Home," whereupon others of the party joined in the chorus with increased volume of sound. As the echo of the echo died away, at the moment of gliding under the shadow of the high mountain, the second verse was begun, but was never finished. If an electric shock had startled every individual of the party, there could have been no more simultaneous effect than when the second line of the second verse was reached, when, instead of song, sobs and outcries of grief poured forth from all lips. It seemed as if there were a tumult of despair mingled with prayer pouring forth without restraint. The rugged boatmen rested upon their oars in awe and gave away in sympathy with the scene before them, until it could truly be said no dry eyes were left nor aching heart but was relieved. Like the downpour of a summer shower that suddenly clears the atmosphere to welcome the bright shining sun that follows, so this sudden outburst of grief cleared away the despondency, to be replaced by an exalted exhilarating feeling of buoyancy and hopefulness. The tears were not dried till mirth took possession—a real hysterical manifestation of the whole party, that ended all depression for the remainder of the trip.

CHAPTER XIII

THE OX TEAM EXPEDITION CONTINUED
THE DALLES, OREGON

I QUOTE FROM MY JOURNAL:

> The Dalles, Oregon, Camp No. 16, March 10. Arrived last night all in a muss, with load out of the wagon, but the mate had his men put the bed on, and a number of willing boys helped to tumble all loose articles into the wagon while Goebel arranged them, leaving the boxes for a second load. Drove nearly three-quarters of a mile to a camping ground near the park, selected by the citizens; surprised to find the streets muddy. Cattle impatient and walked very fast, necessitating my tramping through the mud at their heads. Made second load while Goebel put up the tent, and went to bed at 10:00 o'clock, which was as soon as things were arranged for the night. No supper or even tea, as we did not build a fire. It was clear last night, but raining this morning, which turned to sleet and snow by 9:00 o'clock.
>
> March 11. Heavy wind last night that threatened to bring our tent down on our heads and which brought cold weather; ice formed in the camp half inch thick; damper of stove out of order, which, with the wind, drove the smoke out of the stove and filled the tent full of smoke, making life miserable. In consequence of the weather, the dedication ceremonies were postponed.

Prior to leaving home I had written to the ladies of the landmark committee that upon my arrival at The Dalles I would be pleased to have their cooperation to secure funds to erect a monument in their city. What should they do but put their heads together and provide one already inscribed and in place and notify me that I had been selected to deliver the dedicatory address and that it was expected the whole city would turn out to witness the ceremonies. But alas, the fierce cold winds spoiled all their well-laid plans, for the dedication had to be postponed. Finally, upon short notice, the stone was duly dedicated on the 12th of March with a few hundred people in attendance with their wraps and overcoats on.

Before leaving Seattle I had the oxen shod, for which I was charged the unmerciful price of $15, but they did such a poor job that by the time I arrived at The Dalles all the shoes but one were off the Dave ox, and several lost off Twist, and the remainder loose, and so I was compelled to have the whole of the work done over again at The Dalles.

This time the work was well done, all the shoes but one staying on for a distance of 600 miles, when we threw the Dave ox to replace the lost shoe, there being no stocks at hand. The charge at The Dalles was $10, thus making quite an inroad upon the scant funds for the expedition. I felt compelled to have them again shod at Kemmerer, Wyoming, 848 miles out from The Dalles, but soon lost several shoes, and finally at the Pacific Springs had the missing shoes replaced by inexperienced hands, who did a good job, though, for the shoes stayed on until well worn.

On the Plains in '52 but few shod their cattle. Many cows were worked, and light steers, and most of the outfits had spare cattle to put in their teams in case one became lame or tender footed. I knew of several tying cowhide shoes on to protect the feet of their cattle, while with others it was pitiable to see the suffering, limping, dumb brutes laboring.

OUT FROM THE DALLES

At 3:30 P.M. on March 14 we drove out from The Dalles. I have always felt that here was the real starting point, as from here there could be no more shipping, but all driving. By rail it is 1,734 miles from The Dalles to Omaha, where our work on the old Trail ends. By wagon road the distance is some greater, but not much, probably 1,800 miles. The load was heavy as well as the roads. With a team untrained to the road, and one, ox unbroken, and no experienced ox driver, and the grades heavy, small wonder if a feeling of depression crept over me. On some long hills we could move up but one or two lengths of the wagon at a time, and on level roads with the least warm sun the unbroken ox would poke out his tongue. He was like the young sprig just out of school, with muscles soft and breath short.

PENDLETON, OREGON

A fourteen-days drive to Pendleton, Oregon, 138 ½ miles, without meeting any success in interesting people to help in the work, was not inspiring. On this stretch, with two assistants, the Trail was marked with boulders and cedar posts at intersections with traveled roads, river crossings, and noted camping places, but no center of population was encountered until I reached the town of Pendleton. Here the commercial club took hold with a will, provided the funds to inscribe a stone monument, which was installed, and on the 31st of March dedicated it, with over a thousand people present (see illustration following). Here one assistant was discharged, the camera and photo supplies stored, a small kodak purchased, and the load otherwise lightened by shipping tent, stove, stereopticon, and other etceteras over the Blue mountains to La Grand.

On that evening I drove out six miles to the Indian school in a fierce wind and rainstorm that set in soon after the dedication ceremonies, on my way over the Blue mountains.

A night in the wagon without fire in cold weather and with scant supper was enough to cool one's ardor, but, when the next morning the information was given out that eighteen inches of snow had fallen on the mountains, zero was reached. However, with the morning sun came a warm reception from the authorities of the school, a room with a stove in it allotted us, and a command to help ourselves to fuel.

THE BLUE MOUNTAINS

Before this last fall of snow some had said it would be impossible for me to cross, while others said it could be done, but that it would be a "hard job." So I thought best to go myself, investigate on the spot, and not "run my neck into a halter" (whatever that may mean) for lack of knowing at first hands. So that evening Meacham was reached by rail and I was dumped off in the snow near midnight, no visible light in hotel nor track beaten to it, and again the ardor was cold—cool, cooler, cold.

Morning confirmed the story; twenty inches of snow had fallen, but was settling, very fast. A sturdy mountaineer, and one of long experience and an owner of a team, in response to my query if he could help me across with his team said, "Yes, it's possible to make it, but I warn you it 's a hard job," and so the arrangement was at once made that the second morning after our meeting his team would leave Meacham on the way to meet me.

"But what about a monument, Mr. Bums?" I said. "Meacham is a historic place with Lee's encampment* in sight."

"We have no money," came the quick reply, "but plenty of brawn. Send us a stone and I'll warrant you the foundation will be built and the monument put in place."

A belated train gave opportunity to return at once to Pendleton. An appeal for aid to provide an inscribed stone for Meacham was responded to with alacrity, the stone ordered, and a sound night's sleep followed—ardor rising.

MEACHAM, OREGON

I quote from my journal:

> Camp No. 3, April 4 (1906). We are now on the snow line of the Blue mountains (8:00 P.M.), and am writing this by our first real out-of-door campfire, under the spreading boughs of a friendly pine tree. We estimate have driven twelve miles; started from the school at 7:00 (A.M.); the first three or four miles over a beautiful farming country, and then began climbing the foothills, up, up, up, four miles and soon again up, reaching the first snow at 3:00 o'clock. The long up-hill pull fagged the Dave ox, so we had to wait on him, although I had given him an inch the advantage on the yoke.

True to promise, the team met us, but not till we had reached the snow, axle deep, and had the shovel in use to clear the way. But by 3:00 P.M. we were safely encamped at Meacham, with the cheering news that the monument had arrived and could be dedicated the next day, and so the snowfall had proved a blessing in disguise, as otherwise there would not have been a monument provided for Meacham. Ardor warming.

But the summit had not been reached. The worst tug lay ahead of us. Casting all thoughts of this from mind, all hands turned their attention to the monument, which by 11:00 o'clock was in place, the teams hitched up, standing near it, and ready for the start as soon as the order was given. Everybody was out, the little school in a body, a neat speech was

* Jason Lee, the first missionary to the Oregon country, with four assistants, camped here in September. 1834, at, as he supposed, the summit of the Blue mountains, and ever after the little opening in the forests of the mountains has been known as Lee's Encampment.

made by the orator from Pendleton, and the two teams to the one wagon moved on to the front to battle with the snow. And it was a battle. We read of the "last straw that broke the camel's back." I said, after we had gotten through, "I wonder if another flake of snow would have balked us?" But no one answered, and I took it for granted they didn't know. And so we went into camp on the hither side of the summit. Ardor warmer.

LA GRAND, OREGON

The sunshine that was let into our hearts at La Grand (Oregon) was refreshing. "Yes, we will have a monument," the response came, and they did, too, and dedicated it while I tarried. Ardor normal.

LADD'S CANYON

I again quote from my journal:

> Camp No. 34, April 11. We left La Grand at 7:30 (A.M.) and brought an inscribed stone with us to set up at intersection near the mouth of Ladd's canyon, eight miles out from La Grand. At 1:00 o'clock the school near by came in a body, and several residents to see and hear. The children sang "Columbia, the Gem of the Ocean," after which I talked to them for a few moments, closing by all singing "America" and we photographed the scene. Each child brought a stone and cast it upon the pile surrounding the base of the monument.

CAMP NO. 34

At this camp, on April 12, the Twist ox kicked me and almost totally disabled my right leg for a month and probably has resulted in permanent injury. Much had to be left undone that otherwise could have been accomplished, but I am rejoiced that it was no worse and thankful to the kind friends that worked so ardently to accomplish what has been done, an account of which follows.

BAKER CITY, OREGON

The citizens of Baker City lent a willing ear to the suggestion to erect a monument on the high school ground to perpetuate the memory of the old Trail and to honor the pioneers who made it, although the Trail is off to the north six miles. A fine granite shaft was provided and dedicated while I tarried, and an inscribed stone marker set in the Trail. Eight hundred school children contributed an aggregate of $60 to place a children's bronze tablet on this shaft. The money for this work was placed in the hands of the school directors. Two thousand people participated in the ceremony of dedication on the 19th, and all were proud of the work. A wave of genuine enthusiasm prevailed, and many of the audience lingered long after the exercises were over. A photograph of the Old Timer was taken after the ceremonies of the dedication (see following), and many a moistened eye attested the interest taken in the impromptu reunion.

OLD MOUNT PLEASANT, OREGON

Sixteen miles out from Baker City at Straw Ranch, set an inscribed stone at an important intersection. At Old Mount Pleasant I met the owner of the place where I wanted to plant the stone (always, though, in the public highway) and asked him to contribute, but he refused and treated me with scant courtesy. Thirteen young men and one lady, hearing of the occurrence, contributed the cost of the stone and $6 extra. The tent was filled with people till 9:00 o'clock at night. The next day, while planting the stone, five young lads came along, stripped off their coats, and worked with earnestness until finished. I note these incidents to show the interest taken by the people at large, of all classes.

DURKEE, OREGON

The people of Durkee had "heard what was going on down the line," and said they were ready to provide the funds for a monument. One was ordered from the granite works at Baker City, and in due time was dedicated, but unfortunately I have no photograph of it. The stone was planted in the old Trail on the principal street of the village.

HUNTINGTON

Huntington came next in the track where the Trail ran, and here a granite monument was erected and dedicated while I tarried, for which the citizens willingly contributed. Here seventy-six school children contributed their dimes and half dimes, aggregating over $4.

After the experience in Baker City, Oregon, where, as already related, 800 children contributed and at Boise, Idaho, to be related later, over

a thousand laid down their offerings, I am convinced this feature of the work is destined to give great results. It is not the financial aid I refer to, but the effect it has upon children's minds to set them to thinking of this subject that has heretofore laid dormant, and to kindle a flame of patriotic sentiment that will endure in after life. Each child in Baker City, or in Huntington, or Boise, or other places where these contributions have been made, feel they have a part ownership in the shaft they helped to pay for, and a tender care for it that will grow stronger as the child grows older.

VALE, OREGON

It was not a question at Vale, Oregon, as to whether they would erect a monument, but as to what kind, that is, what kind of stone. Local pride prevailed, and a shaft was erected out of local material which was not so suitable as granite, but the spirit of the people was manifested. Exactly seventy school children contributed to the fund for erecting this monument, which was placed on the court house grounds, and participated in the exercises of dedication on April 30.

CHAPTER XIV

THE OX TEAM MONUMENT EXPEDITION CONTINUED OLD FORT BOISE

THIS FINISHED THE WORK IN OREGON, as we soon crossed Snake River just below the mouth of Boise and were landed on the historic spot of the old Fort Boise, established by the Hudson Bay Company in September, 1834. This fort was established for the purpose of preventing the success of the American venture at Fort Hull, a post established earlier in 1834 by Nathaniel J. Wythe. AVythe's venture proved disastrous, and the fort soon passed into his rival's hands, the Hudson Bay Company, thus for the time being securing undisputed British rule for the whole of that vast region known as the Inland Empire. Some relics of the old fort at Boise were secured, arrangements made for planting a double inscribed stone to mark the site of the fort and the Trail, and afterwards, through the liberality of the citizens of Boise City, a stone was shipped and doubtless before this put in place.

PARMA, IDAHO

The first town encountered in Idaho wasi Parma, where the contributions warranted shipping an inscribed stone from Boise City, which was done, and is doubtless ere this in place, but no photograph of it is at hand.

BOISE, IDAHO

At Boise, the capital city of Idaho, there were nearly 1,200 contributions to the monument fund by the pupils of the public schools, each child signing his or her name to the roll, showing the school and grade to which the child belonged. These rolls with printed headings were collected, bound together, and deposited with the archives of the Pioneer Society historical collection for future reference and as a part of the history of the monument. Each child was given a signed certificate showing the amount of the contribution. The monument stands on the state house grounds and is inscribed as the children's offering to the memory of the pioneers. Near three thousand people attended the dedication service, the program of which is here given in full to show the spirit prevailing and to illustrate the zeal manifested in many other places:

PROGRAM PIONEER MONUMENT DEDICATION
CAPITOL GROUNDS, BOISE, IDAHO,
WEDNESDAY, MAY 9, 1906.
MAJOR J. A. PINNEY, PRESIDING.

Song .... "Idaho"
by the School Children

A lovely mountain home is ours,
Idaho, O, Idaho!
Of winters mild and springtime showers,
Idaho, O, Idaho!
Her breezes blow from western shore;
Where broad Pacific's billows roar;
Each year we love her more and more,
Idaho, O, Idaho!

Her mountains grand are crowned with snow,
Idaho, O, Idaho!
And valleys fertile spread below,
Idaho, O, Idaho!
The towering pines on cliffs so steep,
O'er cataracts their vigils keep,
Or in the lakes are mirrored deep,
Idaho, O, Idaho!

A thousand hills where herds may range,
Idaho, O, Idaho!
And lava beds so weird and strange,
Idaho, O, Idaho!
Above our heads are cloudless skies,
In gorgeous hues the sunset dies.
The starry diamonds greet the eyes,
Idaho, O, Idaho!

Such is our wondrous mountain home,
Idaho, O, Idaho!
And far away we ne'er would roam,
Idaho, O, Idaho!
Oh "Land of Liberty," we tell,
Beneath a starry flag we dwell;
One star is ours, we love it well,
Idaho. O, Idaho!

Invocation . . . . .by Dean Hinks
Address . . . . by F. R. Coffin
Unveiling Monument . . . .
Esther Gregory, Louise Morrison, Edna Perrault, and Elizabeth Hays.

Song . . . ."Star Spangled Banner"
by male quartet composed of
P. E. Tate, C. R. Davis, L. W. Thrailkill, and M. R. McFerrin.

Presentation on behalf of the school . . . . Prof. J. E. Williamson
Address . . . . by Ezra Meeker
The "Trail Marker," of Puyallup, Wash.

Hymn . . . ."America"
by the Audience

My country, 'tis of thee.
Sweet land of liberty—
Of thee I sing:
Land where my fathers died.
Land of the pilgrims' pride.
From every mountain side
Let freedom ring!

My native country, thee—
Land of the noble, free—
Thy name I love:
I love thy rocks and rills,
Thy woods and templed hills;
My heart with rapture thrills
Like that above.

Our fathers' God, to thee.
Author of liberty—
To thee we sing:
Long may our land be bright
With freedom's holy light;
Protect us by thy might.
Great God, our King.

The citizens of Boise also paid for the stone planted on the site of the old fort and also for one planted on the Trail, near the South Boise school buildings, all of which were native granite shafts of which there is a large supply very suitable for such work.

TWIN FALLS, IDAHO

At Twin Falls, 537 miles out from The Dalles, funds were contributed to place an inscribed stone in the track of the old Trail a mile from the city, and a granite shaft was accordingly ordered.

AMERICAN FALLS, IDAHO

Upon my arrival at American Falls, Idaho, 649 miles out from The Dalles, a combination was quickly formed to erect a cement shaft twelve feet high to plant in the track of the Trail, and a park was to be dedicated where the monument is to stand and a section of the old Trail preserved.

POCATELLO, IDAHO.

The ladies' study club has undertaken the work to erect a monument at Pocatello, Idaho, 676 miles out from The Dalles. I made twenty-three addresses to the school children on behalf of the work before leaving, and have the satisfaction of knowing the undertaking has been vigorously prosecuted, and that a fine monument will soon be in place on the high school grounds.

SODA SPRINGS, IDAHO

At Soda Springs, 739 miles from The Dalles, the next place where an attempt was made to erect a monument, a committee of citizens undertook the work, collected the funds to erect a monument by one of those beautiful bubbling soda springs, which is in the park and on the Trail.

MONTPELIER, IDAHO

Montpelier proved no exception to what apparently had become the rule. A committee of three was appointed by the commercial club to take charge of the work of erecting a monument, a contribution from members and citizens solicited, nearly $30 collected and paid into the bank, and arrangements made for increasing the contributions and completing the monument were made before the team arrived.

A pleasant feature of the occasion was the calling of a meeting of the woman's club at the Hunter Hotel, where I was stopping, and a resolution passed to thoroughly canvass the town for aid in the work, and to interest the school children.

THE MAD BULL

I quote from my journal:

> June 7, up at 4:30; started at 5:30; arrived at Montpelier 11:00 A.M. . . . A dangerous and exciting incident occurred this forenoon when a vicious bull attacked the team, first from one side and then the other, getting in between the oxen and causing them to nearly upset the wagon. I was finally thrown down in the meleé, but escaped unharmed, and it was a narrow escape from being run over by both team and wagon.

THE WOUNDED BUFFALO

This incident reminded me of a "scrape" one of our neighboring trains got into on the Platte in 1852 with a wounded buffalo. The train had encountered a large herd feeding and traveling at right angles to the road. The older heads of the party, fearing a stampede of their teams, had given orders not to molest the buffaloes, but to give their whole attention to care of the teams.

But one impulsive young fellow would not be restrained and fired into the herd and wounded a large bull. Either in anger or from confusion the mad bull charged upon a wagon filled with women and children and drawn by a team of mules. He became entangled in the harness and on the tongue between the mules. An eye-witness described the scene as "exciting for awhile." It would be natural for the women to scream, the children to cry, and the men to halloa, but the practical question was how to dispatch the bull without shooting the mules as well. What with multiplicity of counsel, the independent action of every one, each having a plan of his own, there seemed certain to be some fatalities from the gunshots of the large crowd of trainmen who had forgotten their own teams and rushed to the wagon in trouble. As in this incident of my own, just related, nothing was harmed and no one was hurt, but when it was over all agreed it was past understanding how it came about there was no loss of life or bodily injury.

COKEVILLE, WYOMING

Cokeville, 800 ¼ miles out on the Trail from The Dalles, and near the junction of the Sublet cut-off with the more southerly trail, resolved to have a monument, and arrangements were completed for erecting one of stone from a nearby quarry that will bear witness for many centuries.

CHAPTER XV

THE OX TEAM MONUMENT EXPEDITION CONTINUED THE ROCKY MOUNTAINS.

FROM COKEVILLE TO PACIFIC SPRINGS, just west of the summit of the Rocky mountains at South Pass, by the road and trail we traveled, is 158 miles. Ninety miles of this stretch is away from the sound of the locomotive, the click of the telegraph, or the hello girl. It is a great extension of that grand mountain range, the Rockies, from six to seven thousand feet above sea level, with scant vegetable growth, and almost a solitude as to habitation, save here and there a sheep-herder or his typical wagon might be discovered. The bold coyote, the simple antelope, and the cunning sage hen still hold their sway as they did fifty-four years ago, when I first traversed the country. The old Trail is there in all its grandeur.

"Why mark that Trail?" I exclaim. Miles and miles of it worn so deep that centuries of storm will not efface it; generations may pass and the origin of the Trail become a legend, but the marks will be there to perplex the wondering eyes of those who people the continent ten centuries hence, ay, a hundred centuries, I am ready to say. We wonder to see it worn fifty feet wide and three feet deep and hasten to take snap shots at it with Kodak and camera. But what about it later, after we are over the crest of the mountain? We see it a hundred feet wide and fifteen feet deep, two tracks or more abreast as like that shown in the illustration, where the tramp of thousands upon thousands and the hoofs of millions of animals and the wheels of untold numbers of vehicles has loosened the soil and the fierce winds have carried it away, and finally we find ruts a foot deep or more, worn into the solid rock until the axles would actually drag on the solid rock, compeling the opening of a new way. "What a mighty movement, this over the old Oregon Trail," we exclaim time and again, each time with greater wonderment at the marvels yet to be seen, and hear the stories of the few yet left of those who saw, felt, and heard.

Nor do we escape from this solitude of the western slope till we have traveled 150 miles east from the summit, when the welcome black smoke of the locomotive is seen in the distance, at Casper, a stretch of 250 miles of primitive life of ye olden times of fifty years ago.

Nature's freaks in the Rocky mountains are beyond my power of description. We catch sight of one a few miles west of the Little Sandy (see illustration) without name. We venture to call it Tortoise Rock, from the resemblance to that animal, with head erect and extended, as seen in the illustration. Farther on, as night approaches, we are in the presence of animals unused to the sight of man.

PACIFIC SPRINGS

I quote from my journal:

> Pacific Springs, Wyoming, Camp No. 79, June 20, 1906, odometer 958 (miles from The Dalles, Oregon.) Arrived at 6:00 P.M. and camped near Halter's store and the P. O.; ice formed in camp during the night . . .
>
> Camp No. 79, June 21. Remained in camp all day and got down to solid work on my new book, the title of which is not yet developed in my mind . . .

Camp No. 79, June 22. Remained in camp all day at Pacific Springs and searched for a suitable stone for a monument to be placed at the summit. After almost despairing, I suddenly came to exactly what was wanted, and although alone on the mountain side, exclaimed, "That is what I want; that's it." So, a little later, after procuring help, we turned it over to find that both sides were flat; with 26 inches face and 15 inches thick at one end and 14 wide and 12 thick at the other, one of Nature's own handiwork, as if made for this very purpose, to stand on the top of the mountains for the centuries to come to perpetuate the memory of the generations that have passed. I think it is granite formation, but is mixed with quartz at large end and very hard. Replaced three shoes on the Twist ox and one on Dave immediately after dinner and hitched the oxen to Mr. Halter's wagon, and with the help of four men loaded the stone, after having dragged it on the ground and rocks a hundred yards or so down the mountain side; estimated weight, 1,000 pounds.

Camp No. 79, June 23. Remained here in camp while inscribing the monument. There being no stone cutter here, the clerk of the store formed the letters on stiff paste boards and then cut out to make a paper stencil, after which the shape of the letters was transferred to the stone by crayon marks. The letters were then cut with the cold chisel deep enough to make a permanent inscription. The stone is so very hard that it required steady work all day to cut the twenty letters and figures, 'The Old Oregon Trail, 1843-57.'

> Camp 80, June 24, odometer 970 ½. At 3:00 o'clock this afternoon erected the monument described previously on the summit of the South Pass at a point on the Trail described by John Linn, civil engineer, as 42.21 north latitude, 108.53 west longitude, bearing N. 47, E. 240, feet from the ¼ corner between sections 4 and 5, T. 27 N., R. 101 W. of the 6th P. M. Elevation as determined by aneroid reading June 24, 1906, is 7450.
>
> Mr. Linn informs me the survey for an irrigation ditch to take the waters of the Sweetwater river from the east slope of the range, through the. South Pass, to the west side, runs within a hundred feet of the monument.
>
> We drove out of Pacific Springs at 12:30, stopped at the summit to dedicate the monument, and at 3:40 left the summit and drove twelve miles to this point, called Oregon Slough, and put up the tent after dark.

The reader may think of the South Pass of the Rocky mountains as a precipitous defile through narrow canyons and deep gorges, but nothing is farther from the facts than such imagined conditions. One can drive through this pass for several miles without realizing he has passed the dividing line between the waters of the Pacific on the one side and of the Gulf of Mexico on the other, while traveling over a broad, open, undulating prairie the approach to which is by easy grades and the descent (going east) scarcely noticeable.

Certainly, if my memory is worth anything, in 1852, some of our party left the road but a short distance to find banks of drifted snow in low places in July, but none was in sight on the level of the road as we came along in June of 1906. This was one of the landmarks that looked familiar, as all who were toiling west looked upon this spot as the turning point in their journey, and that they had left the worst of the trip behind them—poor, innocent souls as we were, not realizing that our mountain climbing in the way of rough roads only began a long way out west of the summit of the Rockies.

CHAPTER XVI

THE OX TEAM MONUMENT EXPEDITION CONTINUED SWEETWATER

THE SIGHT OF SWEETWATER RIVER, twenty miles out from the Pass, revived many pleasant memories and some sad. I could remember the sparkling, clear water, the green skirt of undergrowth along the banks and the restful camps as we trudged along up the stream so many years ago. And now I see the same channel, the same hills, and apparently the same waters swiftly passing; but where are the campfires; where the herds of gaunt cattle; where the sound of the din of bells; the hallowing for lost children; the cursing of irate ox drivers; the pleading for mercy from some humane dame for the half-famished dumb brute; the harsh sounds from some violin in camp; the merry shout of thoughtless children; or the little groups off on the hillside to bury the dead? All gone. An oppressive silence prevailed as we drove down to the river and pitched camp within a few feet of the bank where we could hear the rippling waters passing and see the fish leaping in the eddies. We had our choice of a camping place just by the skirt of refreshing green brush with an opening to give full view of the river. Not so in '52 with hundreds of camps ahead of you. One must take what he could get, and that in many cases would be far back from the water and removed from other conveniences.

The sight and smell of the carrion so common in camping places in our first trip was gone; no bleached bones even showed where the exhausted dumb brute had died; the graves of the dead emigrants had all been leveled by the hoofs of stock and the lapse of time. "What a mighty change!" I exclaimed. We had been following the old Trail for nearly 150 miles on the west slope of the mountains with scarce a vestige of civilization. Out of sight and hearing of railroads, telegraphs, or telephones and nearly a hundred miles without a postoflftce. It is a misnomer to call it a "slope." It is nearly as high an altitude a hundred miles west of the summit as the summit itself. The country remains as it was fifty-four years before. The Trail is there to be seen miles and miles ahead, worn bare and deep, with but one narrow track where there used to be a dozen, and with the beaten path so solid that vegetation has not yet recovered from the scourge of passing hoofs and tires of wagon years ago.

Like as in 1852 when the summit was passed I felt that ray task was much more than half done, though the distance was scarcely half compassed. I felt we were entitled to a rest even though it was a solitude, and so our preparations were made for two days' rest if not recreation. The two days passed and we saw but three persons. We traveled a week on this stretch, to encounter five persons only, and to see but one wagon, but our guide to point the way was at hand all the time—a pioneer way a hundred feet wide and in places ten feet deep, we could not mistake. Our way from this Camp No. 81 on Sweetwater led us from the river and over hills for fifty miles before we were back to the river again. Not so my Trail of '52, for then we followed the river closer and crossed it several times, while part of the people went over the hills and made the second trail. It was on this last stretch we set our 1,000 mile post as we reached nearly the summit of a very long hill, eighteen miles west of where we again encountered the river, saw a telegraph line, and a road where more than one wagon a week passed as like that we had been following so long.

SPLIT ROCK

I quote from my journal:

> Camp No. 85, June 30, odometer 1,044.
>
> About 10:00 o'clock encountered a large number of big flies that ran the cattle nearly wild. We fought them off as best we could. I stood on the wagon tongue for miles so I could reach them with the whip stock. The cattle were so excited, we did not stop at noon, finding water on the way, but drove on through by 2:30 and camped for the day at a farm house, the Split Rock post office, the first we had found since leaving Pacific Springs, the other side the summit of South Pass and eighty-five miles distant.
>
> Split Rock post office derives its name from a rift in the mountain a thousand feet or more high, as though a part of the range had been bodily moved a rod or so, leaving this perpen-

dicular chasm through the range, which was narrow. This is the first farmhouse we have seen, and near by the first attempt at farming this side (east) of the Rocky Mountains.

CHAPTER XVII

THE OX TEAM MONUMENT EXPEDITION CONTINUED THE DEVIL'S GATE.

THE DEVIL'S GATE and Independence Rock a few miles distant are probably the two best known landmarks on the Trail—the one for its grotesque and striking scenic effect. Here, as at Split Rock, the mountain seems as if it had been split apart, leaving an opening a few rods wide and nearly five hundred feet high, through which the Sweetwater river pours as a veritable torrent. The river first approaches to within a few hundred feet of the gap, and then suddenly curves away from it, and after winding through the valley for half a mile or so, a quarter of a mile distant, it takes a straight shoot and makes the plunge through the canyon. Those who have had the impression they drove their teams through this gap are simply mistaken, for it's a feat no mortal man has done or can do, no more than they could drive up the falls of the Niagara.

This year, on my 1906 trip I did clamber through on the left bank, over boulders head high, under shelving rocks where the sparrows' nests were in full possession, and ate some ripe wild gooseberries from the bushes growing on the border of the river, and plucked some beautiful wild roses, this on the 2nd day of July, A.D. 1906. I wonder why those wild roses grow there where nobody will see them? Why these sparrows' nests? Why did this river go through this gorge instead of breaking the barrier a little to the south where the easy road runs? These questions run through my mind, and why I know not. The gap through the mountains looked familiar as I spied it from the distance, but the road-bed to the right I had forgotten. I longed to see this place, for here, somewhere under the sands, lies all that was mortal of a brother, Clark Meeker, drowned in the Sweetwater in 1854 while attempting to crpss the Plains; would I be able to see and identify the grave? No.

I quote from my journal:

> Camp No. 86, July 2, odometer 1,059. This camp is at Tom Sun's place, the Sun post office, Wyoming, and is in S. 35, T. 29 N., R. 87, 6 P. M. and it is one-half mile to the upper end of the Devil's Gate, through which the Sweetwater runs. The passage is not more than 100 feet wide and is 1,300 feet through with walls 483 feet at highest point. The altitude is 5,860.27, according to the United States geological survey marks. It is one of nature's marvels, this rift in the mountain to let the waters of the Sweetwater through. Mr. Tom Sun, or Thompson, has lived here thirty-odd years and says there are numerous graves of the dead pioneers, but all have been leveled by the tramp of stock, 225,000 of cattle alone having passed over the Trail in 1882 and in some single years over half a million sheep. But the Trail is deserted now.

Scarcely five wagons pass in a week with part of the road-bed grown up in grass. That mighty movement, tide shall we call it, of suffering humanity first going west, accompanied and afterwards followed by hundreds of thousands of stock, with the mightier ebb of millions upon millions of returning cattle and sheep going east, has all ceased, and now the road is a solitude save a few struggling wagons, or here and there a local flock driven to pasture. Small wonder we look in vain for the graves of the dead with this great throng passing and repassing.

A pleasant little anecdote is told by his neighbors of the odd name of "Tom Sun," borne by that sturdy yeoman (a Swede, I think) whose fame for fair dealing and liberality I could hear of upon all sides. The story runs that when he first went to the bank, then and now sixty miles away to deposit, the cashier asked his name and received the reply Thompson, emphasizing the last syllable pronounced with so much emphasis, that it was written Tom Sun and from necessity a check had to be so signed. The name became generally known as such and finally a post office was named after it.

CHAPTER XVIII

THE OX TEAM MONUMENT EXPEDITION CONTINUED INDEPENDENCE ROCK.

CAMP NO. 87, JULY 3, 1906, odometer 1,065, Independence Rock. We drove over to the "Rock" from the "Devil's Gate," a distance of six miles, and camped at 10:00 o'clock for the day.

Not being conversant with the work done by others to perpetuate their names on this famous boulder that covers nearly forty acres and is a mile around it, we groped our way among the inscriptions to find most of them nearly obliterated and many legible only in part, showing how impotent the efforts of individuals to perpetuate the memory of their own names, and, may I not add, how foolish it is, in most cases, forgetting as these individuals have, that it is actions, not words, even if engraved upon stone, that carry one's name down to future generations. We walked all the way around the stone, which, as I have said, was nearly a mile around, of irregular shape, and about one hundred feet high, the walls being so precipitous as to prevent ascending to the top except in a couple of vantage points. Unfortunately, we missed the Fremont inscription made in 1842.

Of this inscription Frémont writes in his journal:

> August 23 (1842), yesterday evening we reached our encampment at Kock Independence, where I took some astronomical observations. Here, not unmindful of the custom of early travelers and explorers in our country, I engraved on this rock of the Far West a symbol of the Christian faith. Among the thickly inscribed names, I made on the hard granite the impression of a large cross, which I covered with a black preparation of India rubber, well calculated to resist the influence of wind and rain. It stands amidst the names of many who have long since found their way to the grave, and for whom the huge rock is a giant gravestone.

> One George Weymouth was sent out to Maine by the Earl of Southampton, Lord Arundel, and others; and in the narrative of their discoveries he says: "The next day, we ascended in our pinnace that part of the river which lies more to the westward, carrying with us a cross—a thing never omitted by any Christian traveler—which we erected at the ultimate end of our route." This was in the year 1605; and in 1842 I obeyed the feeling of early travelers, and left the impression of the cross deeply engraved on the vast rock 1,000 miles beyond the Mississippi, to which discoverers have given the national name of Rock Independence.

The reader will note that Frémont writes in 1842 of the name, "to which discoverers have given the national name of Independence Rock," showing that the naming of the Rock long antedated his visit, as he had inscribed the cross "amidst the names of many."

Of recent years the traveled road leads to the left of the Rock, going eastward, instead of to the right and nearer the left bank of the Sweetwater, as in early years; and so I selected a spot on the westward sloping face of the stone for the inscription, "Old Oregon Trail, 1843-57," near the present traveled road where people can see it, as shown in the illustration opposite, and inscribed it with as deep cut letters as we could make with a dulled cold chisel, and painted the sunken letters with the best of sign writers' paint in oil. On this expedition, where possible, 1 have in like manner inscribed a number of boulders, with paint only, which, it is to be hoped, before the life of the paint has gone out, may find loving hands to inscribe deep into the stone; but here on this huge boulder I hope the inscription may last for centuries, though not as deeply cut as I would have liked had we but had suitable tools.

FISH CREEK

Eleven miles out from Independence Rock we nooued on the bank of a small stream, well named Fish Creek, for it literally swarmed with fish of suitable size for the pan, but they would not bite, and we had no appliances for catching with a net, and so consoled ourselves with the exclamation they were suckers only, and we did n't care, but I came away with the feeling that maybe we were "suckers" ourselves for having wet a blanket in the attempt to seine them, got into the water over boot top deep, and worked all the noon hour instead of resting as like an elderly person should and as like the oxen did.

NORTH PLATTE RIVER

Our next camp brought us to the North Platte River, fifteen miles above the town of Casper.

I quote from my journal:

> Camp No. 89, North Platte river, July 5, 1906, odometer 1,104, distance traveled twenty-two miles.
>
> We followed the old Trail till near 4:00 P.M. and then came to the forks of the traveled road, with the Trail untraveled by any one going straight ahead between the two roads. I took the right-hand road, fearing the other led off too far north, and anyway the one taken would lead us to the North Platte river; and on the old Trail there would be no water, as we were informed, until we reached Casper. We did not arrive at the Platte river until after dark, and then found there was no feed;

got some musty alfalfa hay the cattle would not eat; had a little cracked corn we had hauled nearly 300 miles from Kemmerer, and had fed them the last of it in the afternoon; went to bed in the wagon, first watering the cattle, after dark, from the North Platte, which I had not seen for over fifty-four years, as I had passed fifteen miles below here the last of June, 1852.

Several times during the afternoon there were threatening clouds, accompanied by distant lightning, and at one time a black cloud in the center, with rapid moving clouds around it made me think of a tornado, but finally disappeared without striking us. Heavy wind at night.

This afternoon as we were driving, with both in the wagon, William heard the rattles of a snake, and jumped out of the wagon and thoughtlessly called the dog. I stopped the wagon and called the dog away from the reptile until it was killed. When stretched out it measured four feet eight inches, and had eight rattles.

CASPER, WYOMING

I quote from my journal:

> Camp No. 90, odometer 1,117 ½, Casper, Wyoming, July 6. At the noon hour, while eating dinner, seven miles out, we heard the whistle of the locomotive, something we had neither seen nor heard for nearly 300 miles. As soon as lunch was over I left the wagon and walked in ahead of the team to select camping ground, secure feed, and get the mail; received twenty letters, several from home.
>
> Fortunately a special meeting of the commercial club was held this evening, and I laid the matter of building a monument before them, with the usual result: they resolved to build one and opened the subscription at once, and appointed a committee to carry the work forward. I am assured by several prominent citizens that a $500 monument will be erected, as the city council will join with the club to provide for a fountain as well, and place it on the most public streetcrossing of the city.

Glen Rock was the next place in our itinerary, which we reached at dark, after haying driven twenty-five and one-fourth miles. This is the longest drive we have made on the whole trip.

GLEN ROCK

Glen Rock is a small village, but the ladies met and resolved they "would have as nice a monument as Casper," even if it did not cost as much, because there was a stone quarry out but six miles from town. One enthusiastic lady said "we will inscribe it ourselves, if no stone cutter can be had."

"'Where there's a will there's a way,' as the old adage runs," I said as we left the nice little burg and said good-bye to the energetic ladies in it. God bless the women anyhow; I don't see how the world could get along without them; and anyway I don't see what life would have been to me without that little faithful companion that came over this very same ground with me fifty-four years ago and still lives to rejoice for the many, many blessings vouchsafed to us and our descendants.

DOUGLAS, WYOMING

At Douglas, Wyoming, 1,177 ½ miles out from The Dalles, the people at first seemed reluctant to assume the responsibility of erecting a monument, everybody being "too busy" to give up any time to it, but were willing to contribute. After a short canvass, $52 was contributed, a local committee appointed, and an organized effort to erect a monument was well in hand before we drove out of the town.

I here witnessed one of those heavy downpours like some I remember in '52, where, as in this case, the water came down in veritable sheets and in an incredibly short time turned all the slopes into roaring torrents and level places into lakes; the water ran six inches deep in the streets in this case, on a very heavy grade the whole width of the street.

I quote from my journal:

> Camp No. 95, July 12, odometer 1,192. We are camped under the shade of a group of balm trees in the Platte bottom near the bridge at the farm of a company, Dr. J. M. Wilson in charge, where we found a good vegetable garden and were bidden to help ourselves, which I did, with & liberal hand, to a feast of young onions, radishes, beets, and lettuce enough for several days.

PUYALLUP–TACOMA– SEATTLE

This refreshing shade and these spreading balms carried me back to the little cabin home in the Puyallup valley, 1,500 miles away, where we had for so long a period enjoyed the cool shades of the native forests, enlivened by the charms of songsters at peep of day, with the dripping dew off the leaves like as if a shower had fallen over the forest. Having now passed the 1,200-mile mark out from The Dalles, with scarcely the vestige of timber life, except in the snows of the Blue mountains, one can not wonder that my mind should run back to not only the little cabin home as well as to the more pretentious residence near by; to the time when our homestead of 160 acres, granted us by this great government of the people, was a dense forest; when the little clearing was so isolated we could see naught else but walls of timber around us; timber that required the labor of one man twelve years to remove it off a quarter section of land; of the time when trails only reached the spot; when, as the poet wrote,

> "Oxen answered well for team.
> Though now they'd be too slow;"

when the semimonthly mail was eagerly looked for; when the *Tribune* would be reread again and again before the new supply came; when the morning hours before breakfast were our only school hours for the children; when the homemade shoe pegs and the home-shaped shoe lasts answered for making and mending the shoes, and the home-saved bristle for the waxed end; when the Indians, if not our nearest neighbors, I had liked to have said our best; when the meat in the barrel and the flour in the box, in spite of the most strenuous efforts, would at times run low; when the time for labor would be much nearer eighteen than eight hours a day.

"*Supper.*" Supper is ready; and when repeated in more imperative tones, I at last awake to inhale the fragrant flavors of that most delicious beverage, camp coffee, from the Mocha and Java mixed grain that had "just come to a boil," and to realize there was something else in the air when the bill of fare was scanned.

MENU

Calf s liver, fried crisp, with bacon.
Coffee, with cream, and a lump of butter added.
Lettuce, with vinegar and sugar.
Young onions.
Boiled young carrots.
Radishes.

Beets, covered with vinegar.

Cornmeal mush, cooked forty minutes, in reserve and for a breakfast fry.

These "delicacies of the season," coupled with the—what shall I call it?—delicious appetite incident to a strenuous day's travel and a late supper hour, without a dinner padding in the stomach, aroused me to a sense of the necessities of the inner man, and to that keen relish incident to prolonged exertion and an open-air life, and justice was meted out to the second meal of the day following a 5:00 o'clock breakfast.

I awoke also to the fact that I was on the spot near where I had camped fifty-four years ago in this same Platte valley, then aparently almost a desert. Now what do I see? As we drew into camp two mowing machines cutting the alfalfa; two or more teams raking the cured hay to the rick, and a huge fork or rake at intervals climbing the steep in(!?line of fenders to above the top of the rick, and depositing its equivalent of a wagon-load at a time. To my right, as we drove through the gate the large garden looked temptingly near, as did some rows of small fruit. Hay ricks dotted tbe field, and outhouses, barns, and dwellings at the home. We are in the midst of plenty and the guests, we may almost say, of friends, instead of feeling we must deposit the trusted rifle in convenient place while we eat. Yes, we will exclaim again, "What wondrous changes time has wrought!"

But my mind will go back to the little ivycovered cabin now so carefully preserved in Pioneer Park in the little pretentious city of Puyallup, that was once our homestead, and so long our home, and where the residence still stands near by. The timber is all gone and in its place brick blocks and pleasant, modest homes are found; where the roots and stumps once occupied the ground now smiling fruit gardens adorn the landscape and fill the purses of 400 fruit growers, and supply the wants of 4,000 people. Instead of the slow, trudging ox team, driven to the market town sixteen miles distant, with a day in camp on the way, I see fifty-four railroad trains a day thundering through the town. I see electric lines with crowded cars carrying passengers to tide water and to that rising city of Tacoma, but seven miles distant. I see a quarter of a million people within a radius of thirty miles, where solitude reigned supreme fifty-four years ago, save the song of the Indians, the thump of his canoe paddle, or the din of his gambling revels. When I go down to the Sound I see a mile of shipping docks where before the waters rippled over a pebbly beach filled with shell fish. I look farther, and see hundreds of steamers plying hither and yon on the great inland sea, where fifty-four years ago the Indian's canoe only noiselessly skimmed the water. I see hundreds of sail vessels that whiten every sea of the globe, being either towed here and there or at dock, receiving or discharging cargo, where before scarce a dozen had in a year ventured the voyage. At the docks of Seattle I see the 28,000-ton steamers receiving their monster cargoes for the Orient, and am reminded that these monsters can enter any of the numerous harbors of Puget Sound and are supplemented by a neat array of other steam tonnage contending for that vast across-sea trade, and again exclaim with greater wonderment than ever, "What wondrous changes time has wrought!" If I look through the channels of Puget Sound, I yet see the forty islands or more; its sixteen hundred miles of shore line; its schools of fish, and at intervals the seal; its myriads of sea gulls; the hawking crow; the clam beds; the ebb and flow of the tide, still there. But many happy homes dot the shore line where the dense forests stood; the wild fruits have given way to the cultivated; train-loads of fruit go out to distant markets; and what we once looked upon as barren land now gives plenteous crops; and we again exclaim, "What wondrous changes time has wrought," or shall we not say, "What wondrous changes the hand of man has wrought."

But I am admonished I have wandered and must needs get back to our narrative 1852-1906.

CHAPTER XIX

THE OX TEAM MONUMENT EXPEDITION CONTINUED FORT LARAMIE, WYOMING

I QUOTE FROM MY JOURNAL:

> Camp No. 99, July 16, Fort Laramie, odometer 1,247. From the time we crossed the Missouri in May, 1852, until we arrived opposite this place on the north bank of the Platte, no place or name was so universally in the minds of the emigrants as old Fort Laramie; here, we eagerly looked for letters that never came—maybe our friends and relatives had not written; maybe they had and the letter lost or dumped somewhere in 'The States'; but now all hope vanished to hear from home till the long journey was ended and a missive reach us by the Isthmus or maybe by a sail vessel around Cape Horn. Now, as I write, I know my letter written in the morning will at night be on the banks of the great river, and so for each day of the year. One never ceases to exclaim, "What changes time has wrought!" What wondrous changes in these fifty-four years, since I first set foot on the banks of the Platte and looked longingly across the river for the letter that never came.
>
> This morning at 4:30 the alarm sounded, but in spite of our strenuous efforts the start was delayed till 6:15. Conditions were such as to give us a hot day, but the cattle would not travel without eating the grass in the road, having for some cause not liked the grass they were on during the night, and so, after driving a couple of miles and finding splendid feed, we turned them out to fill up, which they speedily did, and thereafter became laggards, too lazy for anything. So after all we did not arrive here till 4:00, and with dinner at six small wonder if we had good appetites.

Locally it is difficult to get accurate information. All agree there is no vestige of the old Traders Camp or the first United States Fort left, but disagree as to its location. The new fort (not a fort, but an encampment) covers a space of thirty or forty acres with all sorts of buildings and ruins, from the old barracks, three hundred feet long, in good preservation and occupied by the present owner, Joseph Wild, as a store, post office, saloon, hotel, and family residence, to the old guard-house with its grim irou door and twenty-inch concrete walls. One frame building, two stories, we are told, was transported from Kansas City at a cost of $100 per ton freight by ox teams. There seems to be no plan either in the arrangements of the buildings or of the buildings themselves. I noticed one building, part stone, part concrete, part adobe, and part of burnt brick. The concrete walls of one building measured twentytwo inches thick and there is evidence of the use of lime with a lavish hand, and I think all of them are alike massive.

The location of the barracks is in Sec. 28, T. 26 N., R. 64 W. of 6th P. M., United States survey.

SCOTTSBLUFF

We drove out from the town of Scottsbluff to the left bank of the North Platte, less than a mile from the town, to a point nearly opposite that noted landmark, Scotts Bluff, on the right bank, looming up near eight hundred feet above the river and adjoining green fields, and photographed the bluffs and section of the river.

Probably no emigrant of early days but remembers Scottsbluff, which could be seen for so long a distance, and yet apparently so near for days and days, till it finally sank out of sight as we passed on, and new objects came into view. Like as with Turtle Rock (see illustration prior) the formation is sand and clay cemented, yet soft enough to cut easily, and is constantly changing in smaller details.

We certainly saw Scottsbluff while near the junction of the two rivers, over a hundred miles distant, in that illusive phenomenon, the mirage, as plainly as when within a few miles of it.

Speaking of this deceptive manifestation of one natural law, I am led to wonder why, on the trip of 1906, I have seen nothing of those sheets of water so real as to be almost within our grasp yet never reached, those hills and valleys we never traversed, beautiful pictures on the horizon and sometimes above, while traversing the valley in 1852; all

gone, perhaps to be seen no more, as climatic changes come to destroy the conditions that caused them. Perhaps this may in part be caused by the added humidity of the atmosphere, or it may be also in part because of the numerous groves of timber that now adorn the landscape. Whatever the cause, the fact remains that in the year of 1852 the mirage was of common occurrence and now, if seen at all, is rare.

The origin of thie name of Scottsbluff is not definitely known, but as tradition runs, "a trader named Scott, while returning to the states, was robbed and stripped by the Indir ns. He crawled to these bluffs and there famished, and his bones were afterwards found and buried," these quoted words having been written by a passing emigrant on the spot, June 11, 1852. As I passed, stories were told me of same import but shifting the time to 1866.

THE DEAD OF THE PLAINS

From the "Bluffs" we drove as direct as possible to that historic grave, two miles out from the town and on the railroad right of way, of Mrs. Rebecca Winters, who died August 15, 1852, nearly six weeks after I had passed over the ground. But for the handiwork of some unknown friend or relative, this grave, like thousands and thousands of others who fell by the wayside in those strenuous days, this grave would have passed out of sight and mind and nestled in solitude and unknown for all ages to come. As far back as the memory of the oldest inhabitant runs a half sunken wagon tire bore this simple inscription, "Rebecca Winters, aged 50 years." The hoofs of stock trampled the sunken grave and trod it into dust, but the arch of the tire remained to defy the strength of thoughtless hands who would have removed it, and of the ravages of time that seemed not to have affected it. Finally, in "the lapse of time," that usually non-respecter of persons—the railroad survey—and afterward the rails came along and would have run the track over the lonely grave but for the tender care of the man who wielded the compass and changed the line, that the resting place of the pioneer should not be disturbed, followed by the noble impulse of him who wielded the power of control of the "soulless" corporation, and the grave was protected and enclosed. Then came the press correspondent and the press to herald to the world the pathos of the lone grave, to in time reach the eyes and to touch the hearts of the descendants of the dead, who had almost passed out of memory and to quicken the interest in the memory of one once dear to them, till in time there arose a beautiful monument lovingly inscribed, just one hundred years after the birth of the inmate of the grave.

As I looked upon this grave, now surrounded by green fields and happy homes, my mind ran back to the time it was first occupied in the desert, as all believed the country through which we were passing to be, and of the awful calamity that overtook so many to carry them to their untimely and unknown graves. The ravages of cholera had carried off thousands. One family of seven a little further down the Platte lie all in one grave; forty-one persons of one train dead in one day and two nights tells but part of the dreadful story. The count of fifty-three freshly made graves in one camp ground left a vivid impress upon my mind that has never been effaced, but where now are those graves? They are now irrevocably lost. I can recall to mind one point where seventy were buried in one little group, not one of the graves now to be seen—^trampled out of sight by the hoofs of the millions of stock later passing over the Trail. Bearing this in mind, how precious this the memory of even one grave rescued from oblivion, and how precious will become the memory of the deeds of those who have so freely dedicated their part to refreshen the memory of the past and to honor those sturdy pioneers who survived, as well as the dead, by erecting those monuments that now line the Trail for nearly two thousand miles. To these, one and all, I bow my head in grateful memory of their aid in this work to perpetuate the memory of the pioneers and especially the 3,000 school children who have each contributed their mite that the memory of the dead pioneers might remain fresh in their minds and the minds of generations to follow.

A drive of seventeen miles brought us to the town of Bayard, 1,338 miles on the way from The Dalles, Oregon, where our continuous drive began.

CHIMNEY ROCK

Chimney Rock is six miles southwesterly in full view, a curious freak of nature we all remember while passing in '52.

The base reminds one of an umbrella standing on the ground, coyering perhaps twelve acres and running, cone-shaped, 200 feet to the base of the spire resting upon it. The spire (chimney) points to the heavens, which would entitle the pile to a more appropriate name, as like a church spire (see illustration), tall and slim, the wonder of all—how it comes the hand of time has not leveled it long ago and mingled

its crumbling substance with that lying at its base. The whole pile, like that at Scottsbluff and Court House Rock further down, is a sort of soft sandstone, or cement and clay, gradually crumbling away and destined to be leveled to the earth in centuries to come.

A local story runs that an army officer trained artillery on this spire, shot off about thirty feet of the top, and was afterwards court-martialed and discharged in disgrace from the army; but I could get no definite information, though repeated again and again. It would seem incredible that an intelligent man, such as an army officer, would do such an act, and if he did he deserved severe condemnation and punishment.

I noticed that at Soda Springs the hand of the vandal had been at work, and that interesting phenomenon, the Steamboat Spring, the wonderment of all in 1852, with its intermittent spouting, had been tampered with and ceased to act. It would seem the degenerates were not all dead yet.

NORTH PLATTE, NEBRASKA

At North Platte the ladies of the W. C. T. U. appointed a committee to undertake to erect a monument, the business men all refusing to give up any time. However, W. C. Ritner, a respected citizen of North Platte, offered to donate a handsome monument of cement base, marble cap, stone and cement column, five and a half feet high, which will be accepted by the ladies and erected in a suitable place.

CHAPTER XX

OBITUARY NOTICE
DEATH OF TWIST

Old Oregon Trail Monument Expedition, W Brady Island, Neb., Aug. 9, 1906, Camp No. 120, odometer 1,536 ⅝. Yesterday morning Twist ate his grain as usual and showed no signs of sickness until we were on the road two or three miles, when he began to put his tongue out and his breathing became heavy. But he leaned on the yoke heavier than usual and seemed determined to pull the whole load. I finally stopped, put him on the off side, gave him the long end of the yoke and tied his head back with the halter strap to the chain, but to no purpose, for he pulled by the head very heavy. I finally unyoked, gave him a quart of lard, a gill of vinegar, and a handful of sugar, but all to no purpose, for he soon fell down and in two hours was dead.

Such is the record in my journal telling of the death of this noble animal, who I think died from eating some poisonous plant.

When we started from Camp No. 1, January 29, Puyallup, Washington, Twist weighed 1,470 pounds. After we had crossed two ranges of mountains, had wallowed in the snows of the Blue mountains, followed the tortuous rocky canyons of Burnt river, up the deep sand of the Snake, this ox had gained in weight 137 pounds, and weighed 1,607 pounds while laboring under the short end of the yoke that gave him fifty-five per cent of the draft and an increased burden he would assume by keeping his end of the yoke a little ahead, no matter how much the mate might be urged to keep up.

There are striking individualities in animals as well as in men, and I had liked to have said virtues as well; and why not? If an animal always does his duty; is faithful to your interest;

industrious—why not call it by the right name, even if he was 'nothing but an ox?'

We are wont to extol the virtue of the dead and to forget their shortcomings, but here a plain statement of facts will suffice to revive the memories of the almost forgotten past of a type so dear to the pioneers who struggled across Plains and over mountains in the long ago.

To understand the achievements of this ox it is necessary to state the burden he carried. The wagon weighed 1,430 pounds, is a wooden axle and wide track with an average load of 800 pounds. He had, with an unbroken four-year-old steer—a natural-born shirk—with the short end of the yoke before mentioned, hauled this wagon 1,776 miles and was in better working trim when he died than when the trip began. And yet, am I sure that at some points I did not abuse him? What about coming up out of Little Canyon over, or rather up the steep rocky steps of stones like veritable stairs, when I used the goad, and he pulled a shoe off and his feet from under him? Was I merciful then or did I exact more than I ought? I can see him yet in my mind, while on his knees holding the wagon from rolling back into the canyon till the wheel could be blocked and the brakes set. Then when bid to start the load, he did not flinch. He was the best ox I ever saw, without exception, and his loss has nearly broken up the expedition, and it is one case where his like can not be replaced. He has had a decent burial, and a head-board will mark his grave and recite his achievements in the valuable aid rendered in this expedition to perpetuate the memory of the old Oregon Trail and for which he has given up his life.

CHAPTER XXI

THE OX TEAM MONUMENT EXPEDITION CONTINUED

WHAT SHALL I DO? Abandon the work? No. But I can not go on with one ox and can not in all this country find another, and I can not lay here. And so a horse team was hired to take us to the next town, Gothenburg—thirteen miles distant, and the lone ox led behind the wagon.

GOTHENBURG, NEBRASKA

Gothenburg, Nebraska, August 10, 1906, Camp No. 121, odometer 1,549. The people here resolved to erect a monument, appointed a committee, and some fifteen dollars contribution was secured.

LEXINGTON

Again hired a horse team to haul the wagon to Lexington. At Lexington I thought to repair the loss of the ox by buying a pair of heavy cows and breaking them into work, and so purchased two out of a band of 200 cattle near by. "Why, yes, of course they will work," I said, when a bystander had asked the question. "Why, I have seen whole teams of cows on the Plains in '52, and they would trip along so merrily one would be tempted to turn the oxen out and get cows. Yes, we will soon have a team," I said, "only we can't go very far in a day with a raw team, especially in this hot weather.' But one of the cows wouldn't go at all; we could not lead or drive her. Put her in the yoke and she would stand stock still just like a stubborn mule. Hitch the yoke by a strong rope behind the wagon with a horse team to pull, she would brace her feet and actually slide along, but wouldn't lift a foot. I never saw such a brute before, and hope I never will again. I have broken wild, fighting, kicking steers to the yoke and enjoyed the sport, but from a sullen tame cow deliver me.

"Won't you take her back and give me another?" I asked. "Yes, I will give you that red cow (one I had rejected as unfit), but not one of the others." "Then what is this cow worth to you?" Back came the response, "Thirty dollars," and so I dropped ten dollars (having paid him forty), lost the better part of a day, experienced a good deal of vexation, and came away with the exclamation, "Oh, if I could but have Twist back again."

The fact gradually dawned upon me the loss of that fine ox was almost irreparable. I could not get track of an ox anywhere nor of even a steer large enough to mate the Dave ox, the one I had left. Besides, Dave always was a fool. I could scarcely teach him anything. He did learn to haw, by the word when on the off side, but wouldn't mind the word a bit if on the near side. Then he would hold his head way up while in the yoke as if he disdained to work, and poke his tongue out at the least bit of warm weather or serious work. Then he didn't have the stamina of Twist. Although given the long end of the yoke, so that Twist would pull full fifty-five per cent of the load, yet he would always lag behind. Here was a case where the individuality of the ox was as marked as ever between man and man. Twist would watch my every motion and mind by the wave of the hand, but Dave never minded anything except to shirk hard work; while Twist always seemed to love his work and would go freely all day. And so it was brought home to me more forcibly than ever that in the loss of the Twist ox I had almost lost the whole team.

Now if this had occurred in 1852 the loss could have been easily remedied, where there were so many "broke" cattle and where there were always several yoke to the wagon. So when I drove out with a hired horse team that day with the Dave ox tagging on behind and sometimes pulling on his halter, and an unbroken cow, it may easily be guessed the pride of anticipated success went out of me and a feeling almost akin to despair seized upon me. Here I had two yokes, one a heavy ox yoke and the other a light cow's yoke, but the cow, I thought, could not be worked alongside the ox in the ox yoke, nor the ox with the cow in the cow yoke, and so there I was without a team but with a double encumbrance.

Yes, the ox has passed; has had his day, for in all this state I have been unable to find even one yoke. So I trudged along, sometimes in the wagon and sometimes behind the led cattle, wondering in my mind whether or no I had been foolish to undertake this expedition to perpetuate the memory of the old Oregon Trail. Had I not been rebuffed by a number of business men pushing the subject aside with, "I have no time to look into it?" Hadn't I been compelled to pass several towns where even three persons could not be found to act on the committee? And then there was the experience of the constant suspicion and watch to see if some graft could not be discovered; some lurking speculation. All this could be borne in patience, but when coupled with it came the virtual loss of the team, small wonder if my spirits went down below a normal condition.

But then came the compensatory thought as to what had been accomplished; how three states had responded cordially and a fourth as well, considering the sparse population. How could I account for the difference in the reception? It was the press. In the first place the newspapers took up the work in advance of my coming, while in the latter case the notices and commendation followed my presence in a town. And so I queried in my mind as we trudged along—after all, I am sowing the seed that will bring the harvest later. Then my mind would run back along the line of over 1,500 miles, where stand nineteen sentinels, mostly granite, to proclaim for the centuries to come that the hand of communities had been at work and planted these shafts that the memory of the dead pioneers might live; where a dozen boulders, including the great Independence Rock, also bear this testimony, and where a hundred wooden posts mark the Trail where stone was unobtainable; the cordial reception in so many places; to the outpourings of contributions of 3,000 school children; to the liberal hand of the people that built these monuments; to the more than 20,000 people attending the dedication ceremonies. And while I trudged and thought I forgot all about Twist, the recalcitrant cow, the dilemma that confronted me, to awake from my reverie in a more cheerful mood. "Do the best you can," I said almost in an audible tone, "and be not cast down," and my spirits rose almost to the point of exultation.

CHAPTER XXII

THE OX TEAM MONUMENT EXPEDITION CONCLUDED KEARNEY, NEBRASKA

AT THAT BEAUTIFUL CITY of Kearney we were accorded a fine camping place in the center of the town under the spreading boughs of the shade trees that line the streets, and a nice green, fresh-cut sward upon which to pitch our tents. The people came in great numbers to visit the camp and express their approval as to the objects of the trip. I said, "Here, we will surely get a splendid monument"; but when I came to consult with the business men not one could be found to give up any time to the work, though many seemed interested. The president of the commercial club even refused to call a meeting of the club to consider the subject, because he said he had no time to attend the meeting and thought most of the members would be the same. I did not take it this man was opposed to the proposed work, but honestly felt there were more important matters pressing upon the time of business men, and said the subject could be taken up at their regular meeting in the near future. As I left this man's office, who, I doubted not, had spoken the truth, I wondered to myself if these busy men would ever find time to die. How did they find time to eat? or to sleep? and I queried, Is a business man's life worth the living if all his wakeful moments are absorbed in grasping for gains? But I am admonished that this query must be answered each for himself, and I reluctantly came away from Kearney without accomplishing the object of my visit, and wondering whether my mission was ended and results finished.

The reader will readily see that I would be the more willing listener to such an inner suggestion, in view of my crippled condition to carry on the work. And might not that condition have a bearing to bring about such results? No. For the people seemed to be greatly interested and sympathetic. The press was particularly kind in their notices, commending the work, but it takes time to arouse the business men to action, as one remarked to me, "You can't hurry us to do anything; we are not that kind of a set." This was said in a tone bordering on the offensive, though perhaps expressing only a truth.

GRAND ISLAND

I did not, however, feel willing to give up the work after having accomplished so much on the 1,700 miles traveled, and with less than 200 miles ahead of me, and so I said, "I will try again at Grand Island," the next place where there was a center of population, that an effort would probably succeed. Here I soon found there was a decided public sentiment to take action, but at a later date—next year—^jointly to honor the local pioneers upon the occasion of the fiftieth anniversary of the settlement around and about the city, and so, this dividing the attention of the people, it was not thought best to undertake the work now, and again I bordered on the slough of despondency.

I could not repeat the famous words, I would "fight it out on this line if it takes all summer," for here it is the 30th of August, and in one day more summer will be gone. Neither could I see how to accomplish more than prepare the way, and that now the press is doing, and sowing seed upon kindly ground that will in the future doubtless bring forth abundant harvest.

Gradually the fact became uppermost in my mind that 1 was powerless to move; that my team was gone. No response came to the extensive advertisements for an ox or a yoke of oxen, showing clearly there were none in the country, and that the only way to repair the damage was to get unbroken steers or cows and break them in. This could not be done in hot weather, or at least cattle unused to work could not go under the yoke and render effective service without seasoning, and so, for the time being, the work on the Trail was suspended.

As I write in this beautiful grove of the "old court house grounds," in the heart of this embryo city of Grand Island, with its stately rows of shade trees, its modest, elegant homes, the bustle and stir on its business streets with the constant passing of trains, shrieking of whistles, ringing of bells, the reminder of a great change in conditions, my mind reverts back to that June day of 1852 when I passed over the ground near where the city stands. Vast herds of buffalo then grazed on the hills or leisurely crossed our track and at times obstructed our way. Flocks of antelope frisked on the outskirts or watched from vantage points. The prairie dogs reared their heads in comical attitude, burrowing, it was said, with the rattlesnake and the badger.

But now these dog colonies are gone; the buffalo are gone; the antelope have disappeared; as likewise the Indian. Now all is changed. Instead of the parched plain we saw in 1852 with its fierce clouds of dust rolling up the valley and engulfing whole trains till not a vestige of them could be seen, we see the landscape of smiling, fruitful fields, of contented homes, of inviting clumps of trees dotting the landscape. The hand of man has changed what we looked upon as a barren plain to that of a fruitful land. Where then there were only stretches of buffalo grass now waving fields of grain and great fields of corn send forth abundant harvests. Yes, we may again exclaim, "*What* wondrous changes time has wrought."

At Grand Island I shipped to Fremont, Neb., to head the procession celebrating the semi-centennial of founding that city, working the ox and cow together; thence to Lincoln, where the first edition of this volume was printed, all the while searching for an ox or a steer large enough to mate the Dave ox, but without avail. Finally, after looking over a thousand herd of cattle in the stock yards at Omaha, a four-year-old steer was found and broken in on the way to Indianapolis, where I arrived January 5, 1907, eleven months and seven days from date of departure from my home at Puyallup, 2,600 miles distant.

CHAPTER XXIII

A CHAPTER FOR CHILDREN

I WILL TAKE YOU into my confidence, little ones, and tell you a few stories, but they shall be true and about my trips across the Plains with ox teams.

Some little ones have innocently asked if these oxen were cows. No, they are steers trained to work, and when they have been taught to work they are called oxen. The names of my team are Twist and Dave, and they are big oxen and the two weigh over a ton and a half.

I have these shod with iron shoes, nailed on just like with a horse, but oxen must have two shoes on one foot so their split hoofs can spread.

I worked cows in my team when I crossed the Plains in 1852, but we still called them cows after they were taught to work. We used to milk cows on the trip in 1852, and put the surplus milk in a can in the wagon, and at night get a nice lump of fresh butter. The jostling of the wagon would churn the milk.

THE ANTELOPES

One day on this trip while west of the Rocky Mountains, in the state of Wyoming, two antelopes crossed the road about a hundred yards ahead of us, a buck and a doe. The doe soon disappeared, but the buck came back to near the road and stood gazing at us in wonderment as if to say, "Who the mischief are you?"

Our dog Jim soon scented him and away they went up the mountain side until Jim got tired and came back to the wagon, and then the antelope stopped on a little eminence on the mountain and we could see him plainly against a background of sky for a long distance.

Another time we actually got near enough to get a snap shot with our kodaks at two antelopes, but they were too far off to make good pictures. Our road led us obliquely up a gentle hill gradually approaching nearer the antelope. I noticed he would for awhile come toward us and then turn around and look the other way for awhile. After awhile we saw what at first we took to be a kid, or young antelope, but soon after discovered it was a coyote wolf prowling on the track of the antelope, and he was watching both of ua. Just then after I had stopped the wagon, six great, big fat sage hens were to be seen feeding not more than twice the length of the wagon away, just like I had seen them in 1852.

Animals and birds, you know, are not afraid of white people at first sight; it 's only after they learn of their danger they become shy, after we h'ave wantonly mistreated them that they mistrust us. This was way out on the Kocky mountains where scarcely any one lives yet, and where the whole face of the country is nearly a mile and a half above sea level.

QUARREL BETWEEN JIM AND DAVE

Animals have their likes and dislikes same as men and boys, and perhaps girls, too. Early in the trip our dog Jim and the ox Dave became mortal enemies. When I walked and drove, Jim would trot along beside me or at least would stay on that side of the wagon, and Twist, being on the nigh side, paid but little attention to him, but let me get into the wagon to drive and Jim would go over on the side next to Dave, and then the quarrel would begin. Once Dave caught him under the ribs with his right horn, which you see by the picture stands straight out nearly, and tossed him over some sage brush near by. Sometimes, if the yoke prevented him from getting a chance at Jim with his horn, he would throw out his nose and snort, just like a horse that has been running at play and stops for a moment's rest. But Jim would manage to get even with him. Sometimes we put loose hay under the wagon to keep it out of the storm, and Jim would make a bed on it, and woe betide Dave if he undertook to take any of it. I saw Jim one day catch Dave by the nose and draw the blood, and you may readily believe the war was renewed with greater rancor than ever. This war was kept up for more than a thousand miles of the trip, and it is only recently they have ceased to quarrel vigorously, but they are not yet friends to this day.

JIM'S ADVENTURE WITH A WOLF

I have no doubt but Jim has traveled over 6,000 miles on this trip. He would run way ahead of the wagon and then come back on the trot, and if I was riding, invariably go clear back of the wagon and come up by Dave, as it might appear, just to pick a quarrel with him. Then at other times he would run off first on one side of the wagon and then again the other, after birds, jack rabbits, squirrels, or anything in the world that could get into motion. One day a coyote wolf crossed the road just a few rods behind the wagon, and Jim took after him. It looked as though Jim would overtake him, and I was dubious as to the result of a tussel between them, and called Jim back. No sooner had he turned than the wolf turned, too, and made chase, and here they come, nip and tuck as to who conld run the fastest. I think the wolf could, but he did not catch up until they got so near the wagon that he became frightened and scampered away up the slope of a hill near by. At another time a young wolf came and Jim played with him awhile, but by and by the little fellow snapped at Jim and made Jim mad, and he bounced on him and gave him a good trouncing.

When the weather got hot, Jim, before we sheared him, would get very warm, and whenever the wagon stopped he would dig off the top earth or sand that was hot so as to have a cool bed to lie in, but he was always ready to go when the wagon started.

ABOUT PUGET SOUND

Now, little ones, I expect you would like to know something about life on Puget Sound, where I have lived so long. Maybe you do not know what kind of a place Puget Sound is anyway, and so I will first tell you, before I tell you about conditions there.

Puget Sound is really an arm of the sea that runs inland for nearly 150 miles and ramifies into channels, around islands and indentures of bays till there is, by actual government survey, more than 1,600 miles of shore line washed by the tides of the salt waters of the Pacific Ocean. This inland sea, as it is sometimes called, is in the northwestern part of the great state of Washington, and on the shores of the Sound are a great number of towns and some cities, where, in the aggregate, more than 300,000 people now live, but where only a few hundred were there when I first saw it.

And now as to conditions of early life I will quote from my book *Pioneer Reminiscences of Puget Sound, The Tragedy of Leschi*, so you may know a little of my life out in that far-off country as well as of my trips out and back with ox teams and cows.

CHAPTER XXIV

EARLY LIFE ON PUGET SOUND
WILD ANIMALS

I WILL WRITE THIS CHAPTER for the youngsters and the elderly wise-heads who wear specs may turn over the leaves without reading it, if they choose.

Wild animals in early days were very much more plentiful than now, particularly deer and black bear. The black bear troubled us a good deal and would come near the houses and kill our pigs; but it did not take many years to thin them out. They were very cowardly and would run away from us in the thick brush, except when the young cubs were with them, and then we had to be more careful.

THE COUGAR

There was one animal, the cougar, we felt might be dangerous, but I never saw but one in the woods. Before I tell you about it I will relate an adventure one of my own little girls had with one of these creatures near by our owa home in the Puyallup valley.

I have written elsewhere about our little log cabin schoolhouse, but have not told how our children got to it. From our house to the schoolhouse the trail led through very heavy timber and very heavy underbrush—so dense that most all the way one could not see, in the summer time when the leaves were on, as far as across the kitchen of the house.

One day little Carrie, now an elderly lady (I won't say how old), now living in Seattle, started to go to school, but soon came running back out of breath.

"Mamma! Mamma! I saw a great big cat sharpening his claws on a great big tree, just like pussy does," she said as soon as she could catch her breath. Sure enough, upon examination, there were the marks as high up on the tree as I could reach. It must have been a big one to reach up the tree that far. But the incident soon dropped out of mind and the children went to school on the trail just the same as if nothing had happened.

The way I happened to see the cougar was this: Lew McMillan bought 161 cattle and drove them from Oregon to what we then used to call Upper White River, but it was the present site of Auburn. He had to swim his cattle over all the rivers, and his horses, too, and then at the last day's drive brought them on the divide between Stuck River and the Sound. The cattle were all very tame when he took them into the White River valley, for they were tired and hungry. At that time White River valley was covered with brush and timber, except here and there a small prairie. The upper part of the valley was grown up with tall, coarse rushes that remained green all winter, and so he didn't have to feed his cattle, but they got nice and fat long before spring. We bought them and agreed to take twenty head at a time. By this time the cattle were nearly as wild as deer. So Lew built a very strong corral on the bank of the river, near where Auburn is now, and then made a brush fence from one corner down river way, which made it a sort of a lane, with the fence on one side and the river on the other, and gradually widened out as he got further from the corral.

I used to go over from Steilacoom and stay all night, so we could make a drive into the corral early, but this time I was belated and had to camp on the road, so that we did not get an early start for the next day's drive. The cattle seemed unruly that day, and when we let them out of the corral up river way, they scattered and we couldn't do anything with them. The upshot of the matter was that I had to go home without any cattle. We had worked with the cattle so long that it was very late before I got started and had to go on foot. At that time the valley above Auburn near the Stuck River crossing was filled with a dense forest of monster fir and cedar trees, and a good deal of underbrush besides. That forest was so dense in places that it was difficult to see the road, even on a bright, sunshiny day, while on a cloudy day it seemed almost like night, though I could see well enough to keep on the crooked trail all right.

Well, just before I got to Stuck River crossing I came to a turn in the trail where it crossed the top of a big fir that had been turned up by the roots and had fallen nearly parallel with the trail. The big roots held the butt of the tree up from the ground, and I think the tree was four feet in diameter a hundred feet from the butt, and the whole body, from root to top, was eighty-four steps long, or about two hundred amd fifty feet. I have seen longer trees than that, though, and bigger ones, but there were a great many like this one standing all around about me.

I didn't stop to step it then, but you may be sure I took some pretty long strides about that time. Just as I stepped over the fallen tree near the top I saw something move on the big body near the roots, and sure enough the thing was coming right toward me. In an instant I realized what it was. It was a tremendous, great big cougar. He was very pretty, but did not look very nice to me. I had just had a letter from a man living near the Chehalis telling me of three lank, lean cougars coming into his clearing where he was at work, and when he started to go to his cabin to get his gun the brutes started to follow him, and he only just escaped into his house, with barely time to slam the door shut. He wrote that his dogs had gotten them on the run by the time he was ready with his gun, and he finally killed all three of them. He found they were literally starving and had, he thought, recently robbed an Indian grave, or rather an Indian canoe that hung in the trees with their dead in it. That is the way the Indians used to dispose of their dead, but I haven't time to tell about that now. This man found bits of cloth, some hair, and a piece of bone in the stomach of one of them, so he felt sure he was right in his surmise, and I think he was, too. I sent this man's letter to the paper, the Olympia *Transcript*, and it was printed at the time, but I have forgotten his name.

Well, I didn't know what to do. I had no gun with me, and I knew perfectly well there was no use to run. I knew, too, that I could not do as Mr. Stocking did, grapple with it and kick it to death. This one confronting me was a monstrous big one—at least it looked so to me. I expect it looked bigger than it really was. Was I scared, did you say? Did you ever have creepers run up your back and right to the roots of your hair, and nearly to the top of your head? Yes, I'll warrant you have, though a good many fellows won't acknowledge it and say it's only cowards that feel that way. Maybe; but, anyway, I don't want to meet wild cougars in the timber.

Mr. Stocking, whom I spoke about, lived about ten miles from Olympia at Glasgow's place. He was walking on the prairie and had a stout young dog with him, and came suddenly upon a cougar lying in a corner of the fence. His dog tackled the brute at once, but was no match for bim, and would soon have been killed if Stocking had not interfered. Mr. Stocking gathered on to a big club and struck the cougar one heavy blow over the back, but the stick broke and the cougar left the dog and attacked his master. And so it w as a life and death struggle. Mr. Stocking was a very powerful man. It was said that he was double-jointed. He was full six feet high and heavy in proportion. He was a typical pioneer in health, strength, and power of endurance. He said he felt as though his time had come, but there was one chance in a thousand, and he was going to take that chance. As soon as the cougar let go of the dog to tackle Stocking, the cur sneaked off to let his master fight it out alone. He had had enough fight for one day. As the cougar raised on his hind legs Stocking luckily grasped him by the throat and began kicking him in the stomach. Stocking said he thought if he could get one good kick in the region of the heart he felt that he might settle him. I guess, boys, no football player ever kicked as hard as Stocking did that day. The difference was that he was literally kicking for dear life, while the player kicks only for fun. All this happened in less time than it takes me to tell it. Meanwhile the cougar was not idle, but was clawing away at Stocking's arms and shoulders, and once he hit him a clip on the nose. The dog finally returned to the strife and between the two they laid Mr. Cougar low and took off his skin the next day. Mr. Stocking took it to Olympia, where it was used for a base purpose. It was stuffed and put into a saloon and kept there a long time to attract people into the saloon.

Did my cougar hurt me, did you say? I hadn't any cougar and hadn't lost one, and if I had been hurt I wouldn't have been here to tell you this story. The fun of it was that the cougar hadn't yet seen me, but just as soon as he did he scampered off like the Old Harry himself was after him, and I strode off down the trail like old Belzebub was after me.

Now, youngsters, before you go to bed, just bear in mind there is no danger here now from wild animals, and there was not much then, for in all the time I have been here, now over fifty years, I have known of but two persons killed by them.

And now I will tell you one more true story and then quit for this time. Aunt Abbie Sumner one evening heard Gus Johnson hallowing at the top of his voice, a little way out from the house. Her father said Gus was just driving up the cows, but Aunt Abbie said she never knew him to make such a noise as that before, and went out within speaking distance and where she could see him at times pounding vigorously on a tree for awhile and then turn and strike out toward the brush and yell so loud she said she believed he could be heard for more than a mile away. She soon saw something moving in the brush. It was a bear. Gus had suddenly come upon a bear and her cubs and run one of the cubs up a tree. He pounded on the tree to keep it there, but had to turn at times to fight the bear away from him. As soon as he could find time to speak he told her to go to the house and bring the gun, which she did, and that woman went right up to the tree and handed Gus the gun while the bear was near by. Gus made a bad shot the first time and wounded the bear, but the next time killed her. But lo, and behold! he hadn't any more bullets and the cub was still up the tree. So away went Aunt Abbie two miles to a neighbor to get lead to mold some bullets. But by this time it was dark, and Gus stayed all night at the butt of the tree and kept a fire burning, and next morning killed the cub. So he got the hides of both of them. This occurred about three miles east of Bucoda, and both of the parties are living in sight of the spot where the adventure took place.

THE MORNING SCHOOL

And now I will write another story for the youngsters, the boys and girls, and the old folks may skip it if they wish; but I am going to relate true stories.

Soon after the Indian war we moved to our donation claim. We had but three neighbors, the nearest nearly two miles away, and two of them kept bachelor's hall and were of no account for schools. Of course, we could not see any of our neighbors' houses, and could reach but one by a road and the others by a trail. Under such conditions we could not have a public school. I can best tell about our morning school by relating an incident that happened a few months after it was started.

One day one of our farther-off neighbors, who lived over four miles away, came to visit us. Naturally, the children flocked around him to hear his stories in Scotch brogue, and began to ply questions, to which he soon responded by asking other questions, one of which was when they expected to go to school.

"Why, we have school now," responded a chorus of voices. "We have school every day."

"And, pray, who is your teacher, and where is your schoolhouse?" came the prompt inquiry.

"Father teaches us at home every morning before breakfast. He hears the lessons then, but mother helps us, too."

"Peter Smith, the neighbor (and one of the group in the old settlers' meeting), never tires telling the story, and maybe has added a little as memory fails, for he is eighty-four years old now."*

"Your father told me awhile ago that you had your breakfast at six o'clock. What time do you get up?"

"Why, father sets the clock for half -past four, and that gives us an hour while mother gets breakfast, you know."

You boys and girls who read this chapter may have a feeling almost akin to pity for those poor pioneer children who had to get up so early, but you may as well dismiss such thoughts from your minds, for they were happy and cheerful and healthy, worked some during the day, besides studying their lessons, but they went to bed earlier than some boys and girls do these days.

It was not long until we moved to the Puyallup valley, where there were more neighbors—two families to the square mile, but not one of them in sight, because the timber and underbrush was so thick we could scarcely see two rods from the edge of our clearing. Now we could have a real school; but first I will tell about the schoolhouse.

Some of the neighbors took their axes to cut the logs, some their oxen to haul them, others their saws and frows to make the clapboards for the roof, while again others, more handy with tools, made the benches out of split logs, or, as we called them, puncheons. With a good many willing hands, the house soon received the finishing touches. The side walls were scarcely high enough for the door, and one was cut in the end and a door hung on wooden hinges that squeaked a good deal when the door was opened or shut; but the children did not mind that. The roof answered well for the ceiling overhead, and a log cut out on each side made two long, narrow windows for light. The larger children sat with their faces to the walls, with long shelves in front of them, while the smaller tots sat on low benches near the middle of the room. When the weather would permit the teacher left the door open to admit more light, but had no need for more fresh air, as the roof was quite open and the cracks between the logs let in plenty.

Sometimes we had a lady teacher, and then her salary was smaller, as she boarded around. That meant some discomfort part of the time, where the surroundings were not pleasant.

Some of those scholars are dead, some have wandered to parts unknown, while those that are left are nearly all married and are grandfathers or grandmothers, but all living remember the old log schoolhouse with affection. This is a true picture, as I recollect, of the early school days in the Puyallup valley, when, as the unknown poet has said:

> *"And children did a half day's work*
> *Before they went to school."*

---

*Smith has died since this was written. He was one of the most respected pioneers, possessed of sterling qualities of manhood. Like Father Kincaid, he was without enemies.

Not quite so hard as that, but very near it, as we were always up early and the children did a lot of work before and after school time.

When Carrie was afterwards sent to Portland to the high school she took her place in the class just the same as if she had been taught in a grand brick schoolhouse. Where there is a will there is a way.

You must not conclude that we had no recreation and that we were a sorrowful set devoid of enjoyment, for there never was a happier lot of people than these same hard-working pioneers and their families. I will now tell you something about their home life, their amusements as well as their labor.

Before the clearings were large we sometimes got pinched for both food and clothing, though I will not say we suffered much for either, though I know of some families at times who lived on potatoes "straight." Usually fish could be had in abundance, and considerable game—some bear and plenty of deer. The clothing gave us the most trouble, as but little money came to us for the small quantity of produce we had to spare. I remember one winter we were at our wits' end for shoes. We just could not get money to buy shoes enough to go around, but managed to get leather to make each member of the family one pair. We killed a pig to get bristles for the waxends, cut the pegs from a green alder log and seasoned them in the oven, and made the lasts out of the same timber. Those shoes were clumsy, to be sure, but they kept our feet dry and warm, and we felt thankful for the comforts vouchsafed to us and sorry for some neighbors' children, who had to go barefooted even in quite cold weather.

Music was our greatest pleasure and we never tired of it. "Uncle John," as everyone called him, the old teacher, never tired teaching the children music, and so it soon came about they could read their music as readily as they could their school books. No Christmas ever went by without a Christmas tree, in which the whole neighborhood joined, or a Fourth of July passed without a celebration. We made the presents for the tree if we could not buy them, and supplied the musicians, reader, and orator for the celebration. Everybody had something to do and a voice in saying what should be done, and that very fact made all happy.

We had sixteen miles to go to our market town, Steilacoom, over the roughest kind of a road. Nobody had horse teams at the start, and so we had to go with ox teams. We could not make the trip out and back in one day, and did not have money to pay hotel bills, and so we would drive out part of the way and camp and the next morning drive into town very early, do our trading, and, if possible, reach home the same day. If not able to do this, we camped again on the road; but if the night was not too dark would reach home in the night. And oh! what an appetite we would have, and how cheery the fire would be, and how welcome the reception in the cabin home.

"One of the 'youngsters,' fifty years old tomorrow, after reading 'The Morning School,' writes:

"Yes, father, your story of the morning school is just as it was. I can see in my mind's eye yet us children reciting and standing up in a row to spell, and Auntie and mother getting breakfast, and can remember the little bedroom; of rising early and of reading *Uncle Tom's Cabin* as a dessert to the work.

"Near where the old log cabin schoolhouse stood our high school building now stands, large enough to accommodate 400 pupils. In the district where we could count nineteen children of school age, with eleven in attendance, now we have 1,007 boys and girls of school age, three large schoolhouses, and seventeen teachers.

The trees and stumps are all gone and brick buildings and other good houses occupy much of the land, and as many people now live in that school district as lived both east and west of the mountains when the Territory was created in March, 1853. Instead of ox teams, and some at that with sleds, the people have buggies and carriages, or they can travel on any of the eighteen passenger trains that pass daily through Puyallup, or on street cars to Tacoma, and also on some of the twenty to twenty-four freight trains, some of which are a third of a mile long. Such are some of the changes wrought in fifty years since pioneer life began in the Puyallup valley.

Now, just try your hand on this song that follows, one that our dear old teacher has sung so often for us, in company with one of those scholars of the old log cabin, Mrs. Frances Bean, now of Tacoma, who has kindly supplied the words and music:

How wondrous are the changes
Since fifty years ago;
When girls wore woolen dresses.
And boys wore pants of tow;
And shoes were made of cowhide,
And socks of homespun wool:
And children did a half day's work
Before they went to school.

Chorus—Some fifty years ago.
Some fifty years ago.
The men and the boys.
The girls and the toys;
The work and the play,
And the night and the day.
The world and its ways
Are all turned around
Since fifty years ago.

The girls took music lessons
Upon the spinning wheel,
And practiced late and early
On spindle swift and reel.
The boy would ride the horse to mill,
A dozen miles or so,
And hurry off before 't was day.
Some fifty years ago.—Cho.

The people rode to meeting
In sleds instead of sleighs.
And wagons rode as easy
As buggies nowadays;
And oxen answered well for teams.
Though now they 'd be too slow;
For people lived not half so fast
Some fifty years ago.—Cho.

Ah! well do I remember
That Wilson's patent stove.
That father bought and paid for
In cloth our girls had wove;
And how the people wondered
Wken we got the thing to go,
And said 't would burst and kill us all.
Borne fifty years ago.—Cho.

CHAPTER XXV

QUESTIONS AND ANSWERS

FROM THE VERY START, questions were asked and answers given, times without number, one might almost say, some quite pertinent while others were prompted from idle curiosity alone and became annoying. A few of these follow to show the drift of the questions, there being but a small percentage that got right down to the pith of the matter without prompting—the erection of monuments and the teaching of history to the younger generation.

The children in particular were very insistent to know all about the expedition, resulting in contributions from nearly three thousand of them to local committees for erecting monuments. Prom the nature of the questions it became evident that but few of the children knew anything about the old Oregon Trail or of the emigration, or what an ox was, whether some wild animal tamed, or a particular species of animals of which they had never before heard. One little five-year-old girl, with large confiding eyes, one day asked my granddaughter, who was traveling with me, "What is your name?" Not receiving an immediate reply, she cuddled up a little closer, and with a look full in the face, said, "Is your name Mrs. Oxen?" I have been gravely asked by grown-up people if those were the same oxen I drove in 1852, some of these in alleged witticism, yet in many cases in thoughtless queries. The example questions follow:

Q. How old are those oxen, daddy? It seems to me this one is quite young.

A. Yes, that ox, Dave, was an unbroke range four-year-old steer when we started. I broke him in on the road, the same as I did in 1852, the difference being the team was all young and unbroken in '52, while this other ox. Twist, was well broken and is seven years old.

Q. Well, where are you going with that rig? It 's been a long time since I have seen the like of it.

A. I am going first to Omaha, following as near as I can the old Oregon Trail, and then drive on through Iowa and Illinois to Indianapolis, Indiana, my real starting point for Oregon in the fall of 1851.

Q. Goodness gracious; you don't expect to drive all that distance with that yoke of oxen? Let me see, how far is it?

A. Yes, I expect to drive the whole distance with this one yoke of oxen. It is nearly 3,000 miles as the wagon road runs.

Q. Well, it 's been a long time since I have seen one of those old-fashioned prairie schooners; 1 inch-pins and all, eh. I declare, there's the tar bucket, too. Well, well, well; it puts me in mind of old times, sure enough. My father drove one of them across the Plains in '51. I was only a chunk of a boy then, but I remember the trip well. Of course this isn't the same wagon you crossed in, in '52, is it?

A. Oh, no; but that hub in the near fore wheel is from a wagon that did cross the Plains to Oregon in 1853. That is the only old woodwork in this wagon, but you will notice all the hub bands and some other parts of the iron work are from old wagons. Yes, the hub bands of the hind wheels don't match the fore wheels. You see I had to use the remnants of three old wagons to get the irons for one, but that is in keeping with what was to be seen on the Plains after people began to abandon their wagons. Others would come along, take a wheel or an axle to strengthen their own with.

Q. Well, 1 never could see what those prairie schooner wagon-beds were made crooked for, could you?

A. No, I can't say that I can, but they came in very handy in crossing rivers. They are fashioned just like a boat, you know, on the bottom, and answer very well for a boat.

Q. But did you ever see people cross rivers in a wagon-box?

A. Yes. I crossed Snake River in two places myself in 1852 in my wagon-box, but that was in an ordinary square box. Yes, I took my wagon over in it, or rather, on it, for the running-gear was run over the box and gradually run out into deep water till the whole was afloat.

Q. Say, Grandpap, you don't expect them cattle to last you till you get to Indianapolis, do you?

A. Why not? Do they look as if they were about given out? That yoke of oxen weighs 170 pounds more than they did when I left home.

Q. Well, that's a fact, they are both good beef. How much did you say they weighed?

A. The last time I weighed them they tipped the scales at 3,217 pounds. When I started from Puyallup they weighed 3,130.

Q. Uncle, what the mischief are you going on this long journey for this way? Why don't you get you a good, brisk horse team or a span of mules? Oh, say, an automobile would be just the thing, wouldn't it?

A. I am going on this trip for a purpose, not for pleasure or comfort. That purpose is to arouse public interest in and to perpetuate the memory of the old Oregon Trail, and to honor the pioneers who made it, by marking the Trail at intersections with present-traveled roads and erecting stone monuments, suitably inscribed, in centers of population. You will agree with me the ox team and old-fashioned outfit at least accomplishes the first object. To do this speedily and effectively I must first arrest public attention, after which I may enlist their sympathy and secure their aid. Would you have known anything about this expedition had it not been for the ox team?

Q. No, I would not, that's a fact.

Where was it you said you were from, Uncle?

A. Puyallup, Washington.

Q. Where did you say it is?

A. Puyallup is in the valley of that name about nine miles southeast of the city of Tacoma, and is on the Northern Pacific railroad, between Tacoma and Seattle, and nine miles distant from Tacoma and thirty miles south from Seattle.

Q. Let me see, what did you say was the name of that place?

This question was so often asked and other kindred questions not only on this trip but elsewhere, I am prompted to draw once more from my work, *Pioneer Reminiscences of Puget Sound,* and quote from my chapter on names in that work written in lighter vein, yet strictly historical, for I did have the experience in New York, as related, and in London likewise, and afterwards on the Yukon river, and in Dawson.

I have another historic name to write about, Puyallup, that we know is of Indian origin—as old as the memory of white man runs. But such a name! I consider it no honor to the man who named the town (now city) of Puyallup. I accept the odium attached to inflicting that name on suffering succeeding generations by first platting a few blocks of land into village lots and recording them under the name of Puyallup. I have been ashamed of the act ever since. The first time I went east after the town was named and said to a friend in New York that our town was named Puyallup he seemed startled. "Named what?" "Puyallup," I said, emphasizing the word. "That's a jaw-breaker," came the response. *How do you spell it?' P-u-y-a-1-l-u-p,' I said. "Let me see—how did you say you pronounced it?' Pouting out my lips like a veritable Siwash, and emphasizing every letter and syllable so as to bring out the Peuw for "Puy," and the strong emphasis on the "al," and cracking my lips together to cut off the "lup," I finally drilled my friend so he could pronounce the word, yet fell short of the elegance of the scientific pronunciation.

Then when I crossed the Atlantic and across the old London bridge to the borough, and there encountered the factors of the hop trade on that historic ground, the haunts of Dickens in his day; and when we were bid to be seated to partake of the viands of an elegant dinner; and when I saw the troubled look of my friend, whose lot was to introduce me to the assembled hop merchants, and knew what was weighing on his mind, my sympathy went out to him but remained kelpless to aid him.

"I say—I say—let me introduce to you my American friend—my American friend from—my American friend from—from—from"

And, when, with an imploring look, he visibly appealed to me for help, and finally blurted out:

"I say. Meeker, 1 can't remember that blarsted name—what is it?"

And when the explosion of mirth came with: "All the same, he's a jolly good fellow—a jolly good fellow."

I say, when all this had happened, and much more besides, I could yet feel resigned to my fate.

Then when at Dawson I could hear the shrill whistle from the would-be wag, and hear:

"He's all the way from Puy-*al*-lup," I could yet remain in composure.

Then when, at night at the theaters, the jesters would say:

"Whar was it, stranger, you said you was from?"

"Puy-al-lup!"

"Oh, you did?" followed by roars of laughter all over the house—all this I could hear with seeming equanimity.

But when letters began to come addressed "Pewlupe," "Polly-pup," "Pull-all-up," "Pewl-a-loop," and finally "Pay-all-up," then my cup of sorrow was full, and I was ready to put on sackcloth and ashes."

CHAPTER XXVI

AUTOBIOGRAPHY OF THE AUTHOR

NO APOLOGY IS OFFERED for this writing although no very apparent reason may appear to call for it. I am aware that the life of an humble citizen is of not much importance to the public at large; yet, with a widening circle of friends following my advanced years, I feel justified in recording a few of the incidents of a very busy life, and of portraying some customs long since fallen into disuse, and relating incidents of early days now almost forgotten.

I was born at Huntsville, Butler county, Ohio, which is about twenty-five miles northeasterly of Cincinnati, Ohio. This, to me, important event occurred on December 29, A.D. 1830, and so I am many ye^rs past the usual limit of three score years and ten.

My father's ancestors came from England in 1676, settled in Elizabeth City, New Jersey, built a very substantial stone house which is still preserved, furnished more than a score of hardy soldiers in the War for Independence, and were noted for their stalwart strength, steady habits, and patriotic ardor. My father had lost nothing of the original sturdy instincts of the stock nor of the stalwart strength incident to his ancestral breeding. I remember that for three years, at Carlyle's flouring mill in the then western suburbs of Indianapolis, Ind., he worked 18 hours a day, as miller. He had to be on duty at the mill by 7:00 o'clock a. m., and remained on duty until one o'clock at night and could not leave the mill for dinner;— all this for $20 a month and bran for the cow, and yet his health was good and strength seemed the same as when he began the ordeal. My mother's maiden name was Phoeba Baker. A strong German strain of blood ran in her veins, but I know nothing farther back than my grandfather Baker, who settled in Butler county, Ohio, in the year 1801 or thereabouts. My mother, like my father, could and did endure continuous long hours of severe labor without much discomfort, in her household duties. I have known her frequently to patch and mend our clothing until 11:00 o'clock at night and yet would invariably be up in the morning by 4:00 and resume her labors.

Both my parents were sincere, though not austere Christian people, my mother in particular inclining to a liberal faith, but both were in early days members of the "Disciples," or as sometimes known as "Newlites," afterwards, I believe, merged with the "Christian" church, popularly known as the "Campbellites," and were ardent admirers of Love Jameson who presided so long over the Christian organization at Indianapolis, and whom I particularly remember as one of the sweetest singers that I ever heard.

Small wonder that with such parents and such surroundings I am able to say that for fifty-five years of married life I have never been sick in bed a single day, and that I can and have endured long hours of labor during my whole life, and what is more particularly gratifying that I can truthfully say that I have always loved my work and that I never watched for the sun to go down to relieve me from the burden of labor.

"Burden of labor?" Why should any man call labor a burden? It 's the sweetest pleasure of life, if we will but look aright. Give me nothing of the "man with the hoe" sentiment, as depicted by Markham, but let me see the man with a light heart; that labors; that fulfils a destiny the good God has given him; that fills an honored place in life even if in an humble station; that looks upon the bright side of life while striving as best he may to do his duty. I am led into these thoughts by what I see around about me, so changed from that of my boyhood days where labor was held to be honorable, even though in humble stations.

But, to return to my story. My earliest recollection, curiously enough, is of my schoolboy days, of which I had so few. I was certainly not five years old when a drunken, brutal school teacher undertook to spank me while holding me on his knees because I did not speak a word plainly. That was the first fight I have any recollection of, and hardly know whether I remember that but for the witnesses, one of them my oldest brother, who saw the struggle, where my teeth did such excellent work as to draw blood quite freely. What a spectacle that, of a half drunken teacher maltreating his scholars! But then that was a time before a free school system, and when the parson would not hesitate to take a wee bit, and when, if the decanter was not on the sideboard, the jug and gourd served as well in the field or house. To harvest without whisky in the field was not to be thought of; nobody ever heard of a log-rolling or barn-raising without whisky. And so I will say to the zealous temperance reformers, Be of good cheer, for the world has moved in these seventy-five years. Be it said, though, to the everlasting honor of my father, that he set his head firmly against the practice, and said his grain should rot in the field before he would supply whisky to his harvest hands, and I have no recollections of ever but once tasting any alcoholic liquors in my boyhood days.

I did, however, learn to smoke when very young. It came about in this way: My mother always smoked, as long as I can remember. Women those days smoked as well as men, and nothing was thought of it. Well, that was before the time of matches, or leastwise, it was a time when it was thought necessary to economize in their use, and hiother, who was a corpulent woman, would send me to put a coal in her pipe, and so I would take a whiff or two, just to get it started, you know, which, however, soon developed into the habit of lingering to keep it going. But let me be just to myself, for more than twenty years ago I threw away my pipe and have never smoked since, and never will, and now to those smokers who say they "can't quit" I want to call their attention t9 one case of a man that did.

My next recollection of scho«l-boy days was after father had moved to Lockland, Ohio, then ten miles north of Cincinnati, now, I presume, a suburb of that great city. I played "hookey" instead of going to school, but one day while under the canal bridge the noise of passing teams so frightened me that I ran home and betrayed myself. Did my mother whip me? Why, God bless her dear old soul, no. Whipping of children, though, both at home and in the schoolroom was then about as common as eating one's breakfast; but my parents did not think it was necessary to rule by the rod, though then their family government was exceptional. And so we see now a different rule prevailing, and see that the world does move and is getting better.

After my father's removal to Indiana times were "hard," as the common expression goes, and all members of the household for a season were called on to contribute their mite. I drove four yoke of oxen for twenty-five cents a day, and a part of that time boarded at home at that.

This was on the Wabash where oak grubs grew, as father often said, "as thick as hair on a dog's back," but not so thick as that. But we used to force the big plow through and cut grubs with the plow shear, as big as my wrist; and when we saw a patch of them ahead, then was when I learned how to halloo and rave at the poor oxen and inconsiderately whip them, but father would n't let me swear at them. Let me say parenthetically that I have long since discontinued such a foolish practice, and that now I talk to my oxen in a conversational tone of voice and use the whip sparingly. When father moved to Indianapolis, I think in 1838, '^'times" seemed harder than ever and I was put to work whenever an opportunity for employment offered, and encouraged by my mother to seek odd jobs and keep the money myself, she, however, becoming my banker; and in three years I had actually accumulated |37. My! but what a treasure that was to me, and what a bond of confidence between my mother and myself, for no one else, as I thought, knew anything about my treasure. I found out afterwards, though, that father knew about it all the time. My ambition was to get some land. I had heard there was a forty-acre tract in Hendrix county (Indiana) yet to be entered at |1.25 per acre, and as soon as I could get |50 together I meant to hunt up that land and secure it. I used to dream about that land day times as well as at night. 1 sawed wood twice to the cut for twenty -five cents a cord, and enjoyed the experience, for at night I could add to my treasure. It was because my mind did not run on school work and because of my restless disposition that my mother allowed me to do this instead of compelling me to go to school, and which cut down my real school-boy days to less than six months. It was, to say the least, a dangerous experiment and one which only a mother (who knows her child better than all others) dare take, and I will not by any means advise other mothers to adopt such a course.

Then when did you get your education? the casual reader may ask. I will tell you a story. When in 1870 I wrote my first book (long since out of print), *Washington Territory West of the Cascade Mountains*, and submitted the work to the eastern public, a copy fell into the hands of Jay Cook, who then had six power presses running advertising the Northern Pacific railroad, and he at once took up my whole edition. Mr. Cook, whom I met, closely questioned me as to where J was educated. After having answered his many queries about my life on the frontier he would not listen to my disclaimer that I was not an educated man, referring to the work in his hand. The fact then dawned on me that it was the reading of the then current literature of the day that had taught me; and I answered that the New York Tribune had educated me, as I had then been a close reader of that paper for eighteen years, and it was there I got my pure English diction, if I possessed it. We received mails only twice a month for a long time, and sometimes only once a month, and it is needless to say that all the matter in the paper was read and much of it re-read and studied in the cabin and practiced in the field. However, I do not set my face against school training, but can better express my meaning by the quaint saying that "too much of a good thing is more than enough," a phrase in a way senseless, which yet conveys a deeper meaning than the literal words express. The context will show the lack of a common school education, after all, was not entirely for want of an opportunity, but from my aversion to confinement and preference of work to study.

In those days apprenticeship was quite common, and it was not thought to be a disgrace for a child to be "bound out" till he was twenty-one, the more especially if this involved learning a trade. Father took a notion he would "bind me out" to a Mr. Arthens, the mill owner at Lockland, who was childless, and took me with him one day to talk it over. Finally, when asked how I would like the change, I promptly replied that it would be all right if Mrs. Arthens would "do up my sore toes," whereupon there was such an outburst of merriment that I always remembered it. We must remember that boys those days did not wear shoes in summer and quite often not in winter either. But mother put a quietus on the whole business and said the family must not be divided, and it was not, and in that she was right. Give me the humble home for a child that is a home in fact, rather than the grandest palace where home life is but a sham.

I come now to an important event of my life, when father moved from Lockland, Ohio, to near Covington, Indiana. I was not yet seven years old, but walked all the way behind the wagon and began building "castles in the air," which is the first (but by no means the last) that I remember. We were going ont to Indiana to be farmers, and it was hore, near the banks of the Wabash, that I learned the art of driving four yoke of oxen to a breaking plow, without swearing.

This reminds me of an after-experience, the summer I was nineteen. Uncle John Kinworthy, good old soul he was, an ardent Quaker who lived a mile or so out from Bridgeport, Indiana, asked me one day while I was passing his place with three yoke of oxen to haul a heavy cider press beam in place. This led the oxen through the front dooryard and in full sight and hearing of three buxom Quaker girls who either stood in the door, or poked their heads out of the windows, in company with their good mother. Go through that front yard past those girls the cattle would not, and kept doubling back, first on one side and then on the other. Uncle Johnny, noticing I did not swear at the cattle, and attributing the absence of oaths to the presence of the ladies, or maybe, like a good many others, he thought oxen could not be driven without swearing at them, sought an opportunity, when the mistress of the house could not hear him, and said in a low tone, "If thee can do any better, thee had better let out the word." Poor, good old soul, he doubtless justified himself in his own mind that it was no more sin to swear all the time than part of the time; and why is it? I leave the answer to that person, if he can be found, that never swears.

Yes, I say again, give me the humble home for a child, that is a home in fact, rather than the grandest palace where home life is but a sham. And right here is where this generation has a grave problem to solve, if it 's not the gravest of the age, the severance of child life from the real home and the real home influences, by the factory child labor, the boarding schools; the rush for city life, and so many others of like influences at work, that one can only take time to mention examples.

And now the reader will ask, What do you mean by the home life, and to answer that I will relate some features of my early home life, though by no means would say that I would want to return to all the ways of "ye olden times."

My mother always expected each child to have a duty to perform, as well as to play. Light labor, to be sure, but labor; something of service. Our diet was so simple, the mere relation may create a smile with the casual reader. The mush pot was a great factor in our home life; a great heavy iron pot that hung on the crane in the chimney corner where the mush would slowly bubble and splutter over or near a bed of oak coals for half the afternoon. And such mush, always made from yellow corn meal and cooked three hours or more. This, eaten with plenty of fresh, rich milk, comprised the supper for the children. Tea? Not to be thought of. Sugar? It was too expensive—cost fifteen to eighteen cents a pound, and at a time it took a week's labor to earn as much as a day's labor now. Cheap molasses, sometimes, but not often. Meat, not more than once a day, but eggs in abundance. Everything father had to sell was low-priced, while everything mother must buy at the store was high. Only to think of it, you who complain of the hard lot of the workers of this generation: wheat twenty-five cents a bushel, corn fifteen cents, pork two and two and a half cents a pound, with bacon sometimes used as fuel by the reckless, racing steamboat captains of the Mississippi. But when we got onto the farm with abundance of fruit and vegetables, with plenty of pumpkin pies and apple dumplings, our cup of joy was full, and we were the happiest mortals on earth. As I have said, 4:00 o'clock scarcely ever found my mother in bed, and until within very recent years I can say that 5:00 o'clock almost invariably finds me up. Habit, do you say? No, not that wholly, though that may have something to do with it, but I get up early because I want to, and because I have something to do.

When I was born, thirty miles of railroad comprised the whole mileage of the United States, and this only a tramway. Now, how many hundred thousand miles I know not, but many miles over the two hundred thousand mark. When I crossed the great states of Illinois and Iowa on my way to Oregon in 1852 not a mile of railroad had been built in either state. Only four years before the first line was built to Indiana, really a tramway, from Madison, on the Ohio river to Indianapolis. What a furor the building of that railroad created! Earnest, honest men opposed the building just as sincerely as men now advocate the public ownership; both propositions are fallacious, the one long since exploded, the other in due time as sure to die out as the first. My father was a strong advocate of the railroads, but I caught the arguments on the other side advocated with such vehemence as to have the sound of anger. What will our farmers do with their hay if all the teams that are hauling freight to the Ohio River are thrown out of employment? What will the tavern keepers do? What will become of the wagoners? A hundred such queries would be asked by the opponents of the railroad and, to themselves, triumphantly answered that the country would be ruined if railroads were built. Nevertheless, Indianapolis has grown from ten thousand to much over a hundred thousand, notwithstanding the city enjoyed the unusual distinction of being the first terminal city in the state of Indiana. I remember it was the boast of the railroad magnates of that day that they would soon increase the speed of their trains to fourteen miles an hour—this when they were running twelve.

In the year 1844 a letter came from Grandfather Baker to my mother that he would give her a thousand dollars with which to buy a farm. The burning question with my father and mother was how to get that money out from Ohio to Indiana. They actually went in a covered wagon to Ohio for it and hauled it home, all silver dollars, in a box—this at a time when there had been but a few million silver dollars coined in all of the United States. It was this money that bought the farm five miles southwest from Indianapolis, where I received my first real farm training. Father had advanced ideas about farming, though a miller by trade, and early taught me some valuable lessons I never forgot. We (I say "we" advisedly, as father continued to work in the mill and left me in charge of the farm) soon brought up the run-down farm to produce twenty-three bushels of wheat per acre instead of ten, by the rotation of corn, and clover and then wheat. But there was no money in farming at the then prevailing prices, and the land, which father paid ten dollars an acre for would not yield a rental equal to the interest on the money. Now that same land is probably worth five hundred dollars an acre.

For a time I worked in the *Journal* printing office for S. V. B. Noel, who, I think, was the publisher of the *Journal*, and also printed a freesoil paper. A part of my duty was to deliver those papers to subscribers who always treated me civilly, but when I was caught on the streets of Indianapolis with the papers in my hand I was sure of abuse from some one, and a number of times narrowly escaped personal violence. In the office I worked as roller boy, but known as "the devil," a term that annoyed me not a little. The pressman was a man by the name of Wood. In the same room was a power press, the power being a stalwart negro who turned a crank. We used to race with the power press, and could print just half as many sheets on the hand press as they could on the vaunted power press, when I would fly the sheets, that is, take them ofif when printed with one hand and roll the type with the other. This so pleased Noel that he advanced my wages to $1.50 a week.

The present generation can have no conception of the brutal virulence of the advocates of slavery against the "nigger" and "nigger lovers," as all were known who did not join in the crusade against the negroes. One day we heard a commotion on the streets, and upon inquiry were told that "they had just killed a nigger up the street, that's all," and went back to work shocked, but could do nothing. But when a little later word came that it was Wood's brother that had led the mob and that it was "old Jimmy Blake's man" (who was known as a sober, inoffensive colored man) consternation seized

Wood as with an iron grip. His grief was inconsolable. The negro had been set upon by rtie mob just because he was a negro and for no other reason and brutally murdered. That murder, coupled with the abuse I had received at the hands of this same element, set me to thinking, and I then and there embraced the anti-slavery doctrines and ever after adhered to them till the question was settled.

One of the subscribers to whom I delivered that anti-slavery paper was Henry Ward Beecher, who had then not attained the fame that came to him later in life, but to whom I became attached by his kind treatment and kind words he always found time to utter. He was then, I think, pastor of the Congregational church that faced on the "Governor's circle." The church doubtless has long since been torn down.

One episode of my life I remember because I thought my parents were in the wrong. Vocal music was taught in singing schools almost, I might say, as regular as day schools. I was passionately fond of music, and before the change came had a splendid alto voice, and became a leader in my part of the class. This coming to the notice of the trustees of Beecher's church, an effort was made to have me join the choir. Mother fii'st objected because my clothea were not good enough, whereupon an offer was made to suitably clothe me and pay something besides; but father objected because he did not want me to listen to preaching other than the sect (Campbellite) to which he belonged. The incident set me to thinking, and finally drove me, young as I was, into the liberal faith, though I dare not openly espouse it. In those days many ministers openly preached of endless punishment in a lake of fire, but I never could believe the doctrine, and yet their words would carry terror into my heart. The ways of the world are better now in this, as in many other respects.

One episode of my life while working in the printing office I have remembered vividly ail these years. During the campaign of 1844 the Whigs held a second gathering on the Tippecanoe battle-ground. It could hardly be called a convention. A better name for the gathering would be a political camp-meeting. The people came in wagons, on horseback, afoot—any way to get there—and camped just like people used to do in their religious camp-meetings. The journeymen printers of the Journal office planned to go in a covered dead axle wagon, and signified they would make a place for the "devil" if his parents would let him go along. This was speedily arranged with mother, who always took charge of such matters. The proposition coming to Noel's ears he said for the men to print me some campaign songs, which they did with a will, Wood running them off the press after night while I rolled the type for him. My! Wasn't I the proudest boy that ever walked the earth? Visions of a pocket full of money haunted me almost day and night until we arrived on the battlefield. But lo and behold, nobody would pay any attention to me. Bands of music were playing here and there; glee clubs would sing and march first on one side the ground and then the other; processions were marching and the crowds surging, making it necessary for one to look out and not get run over. Coupled with this, the rain would pour down in torrents, but the marching and countermarching went on all the same and continued for a week. An elderly journeyman printer named May, who in a way stood sponsor for our party, told me if I would get up on the fence and sing my songs the people would buy them, and sure enough the crowds came and I sold every copy I had, and went home with eleven dollars in my pocket, the richest boy on earth.

It was about this time the start was made of printing the *Indianapolis News*, a paper that has thriven all these after years. These same rollicking printers that comprised the party to the battle-ground put their heads together to have some fun, and began printing out of hours a small 9 x 11 sheet filled with short paragraphs of sharp sayings of men and things about town, some more expressive than elegant, and in fact some not fit for polite ears; but the pith of the matter was they treated only of things that were true and of men moving in the highest circles. I can not recall the given names of any of these men. May, the elderly man before referred to, a man named Finly, and another. Elder, were the leading spirits in the enterprise. Wood did the presswork and my share was to ink the type, and in part stealthily distribute the papers, for it was a great secret where they came from at the start—all this "just for the fun of the thing," but the sheet caused so much comment and became sought after so much that the mask was thrown off and the little paper launched as a "semi-occasional" publication and "sold by carrier only," all this by after hours, when the regular day's work was finished. I picked up quite a good many fip-i-na-bits (a coin representing the value of 6¼ cents) myself from the sale of these. After awhile the paper was published regularly, a rate established, and the little paper took its place among the regular publications of the day. This writing is altogether from memory of occurrences sixty-two years ago, and may be faulty in detail, but the main facts are true, which probably will be borne out by the files of the great newspaper that has grown from the seed sown by those restless journeymen printers.

This writing has already run far beyond the space allotted for it, and must necessarily be suspended until a more opportune time.

Horace Greeley, writing of the resumption of specie payment, said the way to resume was to resume, and applying that rule, the way to suspend this writing is to suspend. So ends this chapter, and so ends the book.

FROM THE NEW YORK EVENING POST, SATURDAY, MAY 18TH, 1907

LAST BLAZES ON THE OREGON TRAIL

Aged Pioneer Retraced his March of Fifty-Four Years Before—Ezra Meeker —Journey from Puyallup to his Indiana Home—Many Monuments Erected Along the Way—Famous Travelers who Trod the Rough Road's 2,000 Miles—Both the Oregon and Santa Fe Trails Now Permanently Marked.

ORIGINALLY BLAZED, for a portion of the way, by De la Verendrye, in 1742; trodden a distance by Lewis and Clark as they pushed across the vast trans-Mississippi empire; worn by the trappers and adventurers of the first quarter of the nineteenth century, such men as Ezekiel Williams, Gen. Ashley, "Tim" Bridger, Campbell, Fitzpatrick, Sublette, and Wilson Price Hunt, and made into a hard and smooth highway by the hardy Missourians rushing across the continent in search of gold, by the Mormons seeking a new land of liberty, and by countless soldiers of fortune, the tamour Oregon trail has at last been rescued from oblivion and marked with stone monuments, thanks largely to the work of one man, Ezra Meeker.

Starting from his home in Puyallup, Wash., on January 29, 1906, Mr. Meeker retraced his march of fifty-four years before, back along the Oregon trail to its Eastern terminus, on the Missouri River, then across Iowa and Illinois to his Indiana home. As he journeyed, Mr. Meeker interested the people along the route in the importance of saving the Oregon trail from oblivion. Their fathers and grandfathers had helped to make it, but the past was in a fair way to be forgotten. The line of a great transcontinental railroad parallels or covers the old Oregon trail for much of its wajr to-day, but there were detours and stages to be marked before they were lost sight of entirely.

So this old trail, which was one of the great roadways of the nation a century and a half-century ago, has become known better than ever to the present generation. Between Puyallup and Omaha nineteen monuments have been erected. Ezra Meeker, after a year's travel, reached his Indiana home. His journey and his work ended. Not so the interest in the old trail, especially as it follows the marking of another old trail, the Santa Fe, through Kansas.

Before tracing the Oregon trail across the country from the Missouri River to the Pacific Ocean and counting over those who wore it smooth, it might be well to summarize briefly Mr. Meeker's work in marking it.

INTERESTING THE PEOPLE

After he left his Washington home, more than 2,500 people contributed to the erection of Oregon trail monuments. At intervals along the route, Mr. Meeker, with the aid of people for whom he and others blazed the way, erected monuments—a huge stone boulder here, a cairn of stones there, a signboard or post in another place. In Baker City, Oregon, the monument was erected by contributions received from 800 school-children, all of whom were present when it was dedicated. At Boise, Idaho, Mr. Meeker camped for several days beside the post office. He spoke to the public school-children of his object, and 1,200 contributed to purchase the granite monument, which will mark the place where the old-timers passed through what is now a thriving city. The governor of the State and other State officers insisted that the monument be erected on the State House yard, and it was dedicated in the presence more than 3,000 people.

To erect a monument at the summit of South Pass, Mr. Meeker travelled eighty-four miles from a post office, and twenty-four persons who reside in the neighborhood were the only witnesses of the event. The monument stands on the irrigation survey near Sweetwater, and is 7,450 feet above sea level, one of the highest of such landmarks in the country.

In many of the towns and places where monuments were erected, Mr. Meeker stayed see the work done, but in many other instances he turned the matter over to a local committee appointed for that purpose.

BEGAN ON THE MISSOURI

The Oregon trail began, as did the Santa Fe trail, leading to the Southwest, at the town of Independence, on the Missouri River. Practically, St. Louis was the eastern terminus, men and goods going up the Missouri River to Independence, and there taking wagon and setting out either for the Northwest or the Southwest.

The two trails were the same for forty-one miles, when, as the historian Chittenden remarks, a simple signboard was seen which carried ttie words. "Road to Oregon." That signboard to-day, with its lack of os-

tentation and its epigrammatic clearness, would be worth more than its proverbial weight in gold to any State historical society.

There were branch trails that came into the road from Leavenworth and St. Joseph: striking it above the point of departure from the Santa Fe trail; but the Oregon trail proper swung off from this fork, running steadily to the northwest, part of the time along the Little Blue River, until at length it struck the valley of the Platte, so essential to its welfare. The distance from Independence to the Platte was 316 miles, the trail reaching the Platte about twenty miles below the head of Grand Island, The course thence lay up the Platte valley to the two fords, about at the Forks of the Platte, 433 or 493 miles.

Here at the Forks was a point of departure in the old days. If one chose to follow the South Forks of the Platte he might bring up in the Bayou Salade, within reach of the Spanish settlements and the head of the Arkansas, or he might take the other arm and come out on the edge of the Continental Divide, much higher to the north.

The Oregon trail followed the South Fork for a time, then swung over to the North Fork, at Ash Creek, 513 miles from Independence. It was 667 miles to Fort Laramie, which was the last post on the eastern side of the Rockies. Thence the trail struggled on up the Platte, keeping close as it might to the stream, till it reached the ford of the Platte, well up toward the mountains, and 794 miles out from independence, nearly the same distance from that point as was Santa Fe on the lower trail.

INDEPENDENCE ROCK

A little farther on the trail forsook the Platte, 807 miles out from Missouri, and swung across to the valley of the Sweetwater. The famous Independence Rock, 838 miles from Independence, was one of the most noteworthy features along the trail. It marked the entrance into the Sweetwater district and was a sort of register, holding the rudely carved names of many of the hardy Western adventurers. By the Sweetwater the Oregon trailers were taken below the foot of the Bighorns, past the Devil's Gate, and up to that remarkable crossing of the Rockies, known as South Pass, where Ezra Meeker dedicated his monument under such unusual circumstances, taking water from the irrigation ditches on the east side of the Continental Divide to irrigate the west side. This is 947 miles from the Missouri River.

Starting now down the Pacific side of the Great Divide, the traveller passed over 125 miles of somewhat forbidding country, crossing the Green River before he came to Fort Bridger, the first resting point west of the

Rockies, 1,070 miles from the Missouri. This was a delightful spot in every way, and always welcomed by the Oregon trailers.

The Bear River was 1,136 miles from Independence, and to the Soda Springs, on the big bend of the Bear, was 1,206 miles. Thence one crossed over the height of land between the Bear and Port Neuf Rivers, the latter being Columbia water; and, at a distance of 1,288 miles from Independence, reached the very important point of Fort Hall, the post established by Nathaniel Wyeth. This was the first point at which the trail struck the Snake River, that great lower arm of the Columbia, which came dropping from its source opposite the headwaters of the Missouri to point out the way to travellers.

At the Raft River was another point of great interest; for here turned aside the arm of the transcontinental trail that led to California. This fork of the road was 1,334 miles from the Missouri. Working as best it might from the Raft River, down the Great Snake valley, touching and crossing and paralleling several different streams, the Oregon trail proper ran until it reached the Grande Ronde valley, at the eastern edge of the difficult Blue Mountains, 1,736 miles from the starting point. The railway today crosses the Blues exactly where the old trail did.

Then the route struck the Umatilla, and shortly thereafter the Columbia River. It was 1,934 miles to the Dalles, 1,977 to the Cascades, 2,020 miles to Fort Vancouver, and 2,134 to the mouth of the Columbia, though the trail proper terminated at Fort Vancouver.

Such was the Oregon trail, traversed by hundreds and thousands of hardy adventurers, outlet of the Missouri rendezvousing station, a mighty highway across which surged the advance tide of a nation's traffic.

BLAZERS OF THE TRAIL

Who blazed and followed this historic highway, destined to be marked to posterity fifty years after its zenith? The Frenchman De la Verendrye was perhaps the first to tread a portion of the later Oregon trail; since it is known that he forsook the Missouri River and started overland, possibly up the Platte, crossing some of the country which the Astorians saw later. This was in 1742. The trapper Ezekiel Williams, said to have been the first white man to cross the borders of what is now Wyoming, followed in the wake of Lewis and Clarke, in 1807, and blazed a part of the way. Andrew Henry, whose name was given to a beautiful lake of the Rockies; Etienne Provost, the probable discoverer of historic South Pass; Campbell, Fitzpatrick, Sublette, Jim Bridger, Gen. Ashley, Bonneville, and Walker; these are but a few of the leaders who blazed and trod the Oregon trail, making it a well-defined highway before Frémont set out as a "pathfinder."

Then came Wilson Price Hunt, with his overland Astorians, seeking a way from the mid-Missouri to the Columbia River. Later, Robert Stuart and the returning Astorians were to mark out, east of the Continental Divide, the route of the trail for much of its length. Then came scores of trappers and traders; then Bonneville and his wagons, to deepen the trail, in 1832: and two years later, in 1834, Campbell and Sublette built old Fort Laramie on Laramie Creek, a branch of the Platte. Eight years later. Fort Bridger was built by Jim Bridger, on a branch of the Green River.

In 1836 two women moved out into the West along the Oregon trail. They were the wives of Whitman and Spalding, missionaries bound for Oregon. Father de Smet, a missionary also, followed in 1840; then more missionaries from New England, and two years later Fremont, as far, at least, as the South Pass.

So the Oregon trail was blazed and tramped; traders, trappers, gold-seekers, missionaries, colonists until the highway stretched from the Missouri River to the Pacific Ocean. Years passed and railroads supplanted the old Oregon trail; its very whereabouts was forgotten; disputes arose. Then an old man, almost eighty, with his grandchild, clambered into a prairie schooner, made in part of the one in which he had journeyed westward in 1852, and the Oregon trail was retraced and marked with monuments, that a people and a nation may not forget.

F. G. M.

www.ingramcontent.com/pod-product-compliance
Lightning Source LLC
Chambersburg PA
CBHW031337060726
47590CB00007B/2515

* 9 7 8 1 6 3 0 2 3 4 0 1 0 *